VICKSBURG EXPEDITION GUIDE

A comprehensive guide to the Siege of Vicksburg

The Vicksburg Expedition Guide is a unique combination of a computer DVD-ROM, a self-guide audio tour, and an illustrated guidebook, designed to take you on an unforgettable journey to the hallowed grounds of the Vicksburg National Military Park.

Special thanks to Terry Winschel and the staff at
Vicksburg National Military Park.

First published in the USA 2002 by TravelBrains, Inc.

Disclaimer

This book is intended for viewing at tour stops only. Please keep your eyes on the road at all times while driving. TravelBrains shall have neither liability nor responsibility to any person or entity with respect to any loss or damage caused, or alleged to have been caused, directly or indirectly, by the use of this product.

Edwin C. Bearss

FEATURING: ED BEARSS

Ed Bearss, the former chief historian of the National Park Service, began his career with the National Park Service at the Vicksburg National Military Park in 1955. Today, Ed is recognized as one of the leading experts on the campaign and siege of Vicksburg. Ed is also a highly sought after speaker on many topics of the Civil War for his ability to entertain and educate at the same time. He has made numerous appearances on popular Civil War documentaries, including, Ken Burns' PBS series *The Civil War* and the History Channel's *Civil War Journal.*

CAUTION: Many people walk along the roads in the park. Please maintain a safe speed and keep your eyes on the road at all times while driving.

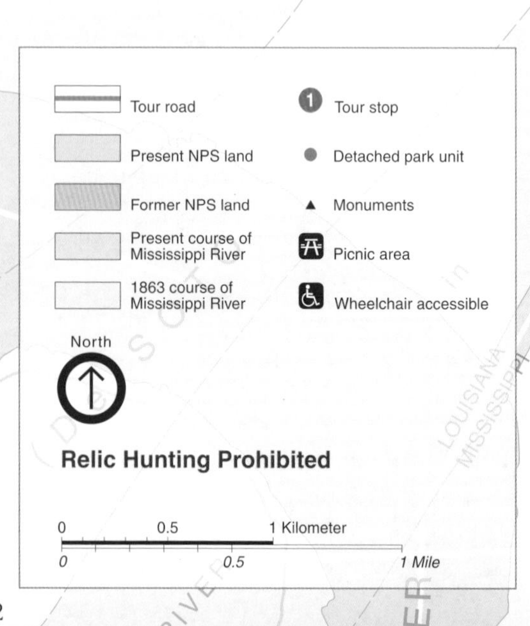

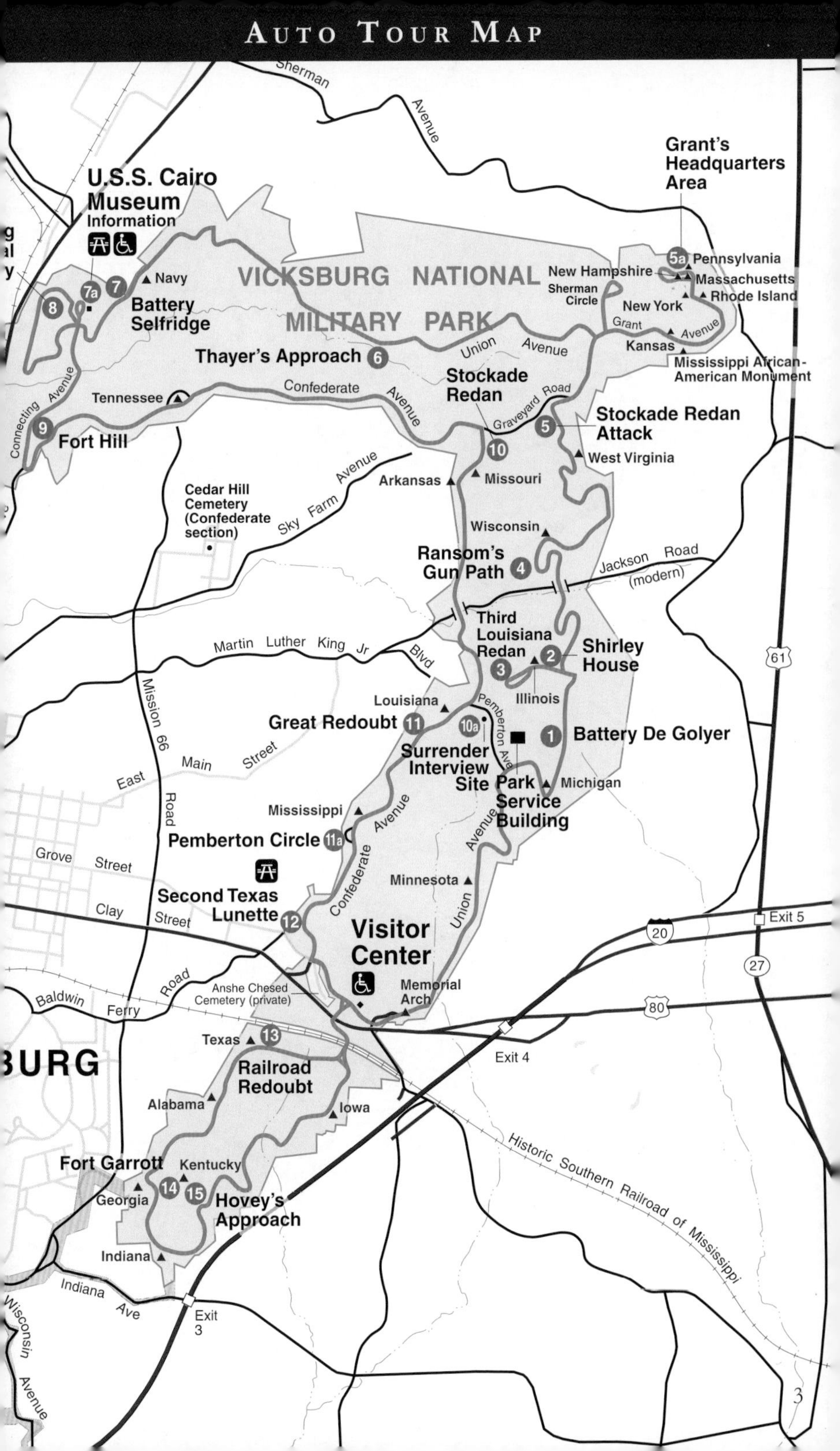

VICKSBURG NATIONAL MILITARY PARK
U.S.S. Cairo Museum
Information
Grant's Headquarters Area
Pennsylvania
New Hampshire
Massachusetts
Sherman Circle
New York
Rhode Island
Grant Avenue
Kansas
Mississippi African-American Monument
Navy
Battery Selfridge
Thayer's Approach
Union Avenue
Stockade Redan
Graveyard Road
Stockade Redan Attack
West Virginia
Tennessee
Confederate Avenue
Connecting Avenue
Fort Hill
Arkansas
Missouri
Cedar Hill Cemetery (Confederate section)
Sky Farm Avenue
Wisconsin
Ransom's Gun Path
Jackson Road (modern)
Third Louisiana Redan
Shirley House
Martin Luther King Jr Blvd
Illinois
Louisiana
Great Redoubt
Pemberton Ave
Battery De Golyer
Surrender Interview Site
Park Service Building
Michigan
Mission 66 Road
East Main Street
Mississippi
Pemberton Circle
Grove Street
Minnesota
Second Texas Lunette
Clay Street
Visitor Center
Memorial Arch
Anshe Chesed Cemetery (private)
Baldwin Ferry Road
Exit 5
Exit 4
Texas
Railroad Redoubt
Alabama
Iowa
Fort Garrott
Kentucky
Georgia
Hovey's Approach
Indiana
Historic Southern Railroad of Mississippi
Indiana Ave
Exit 3
Wisconsin Avenue

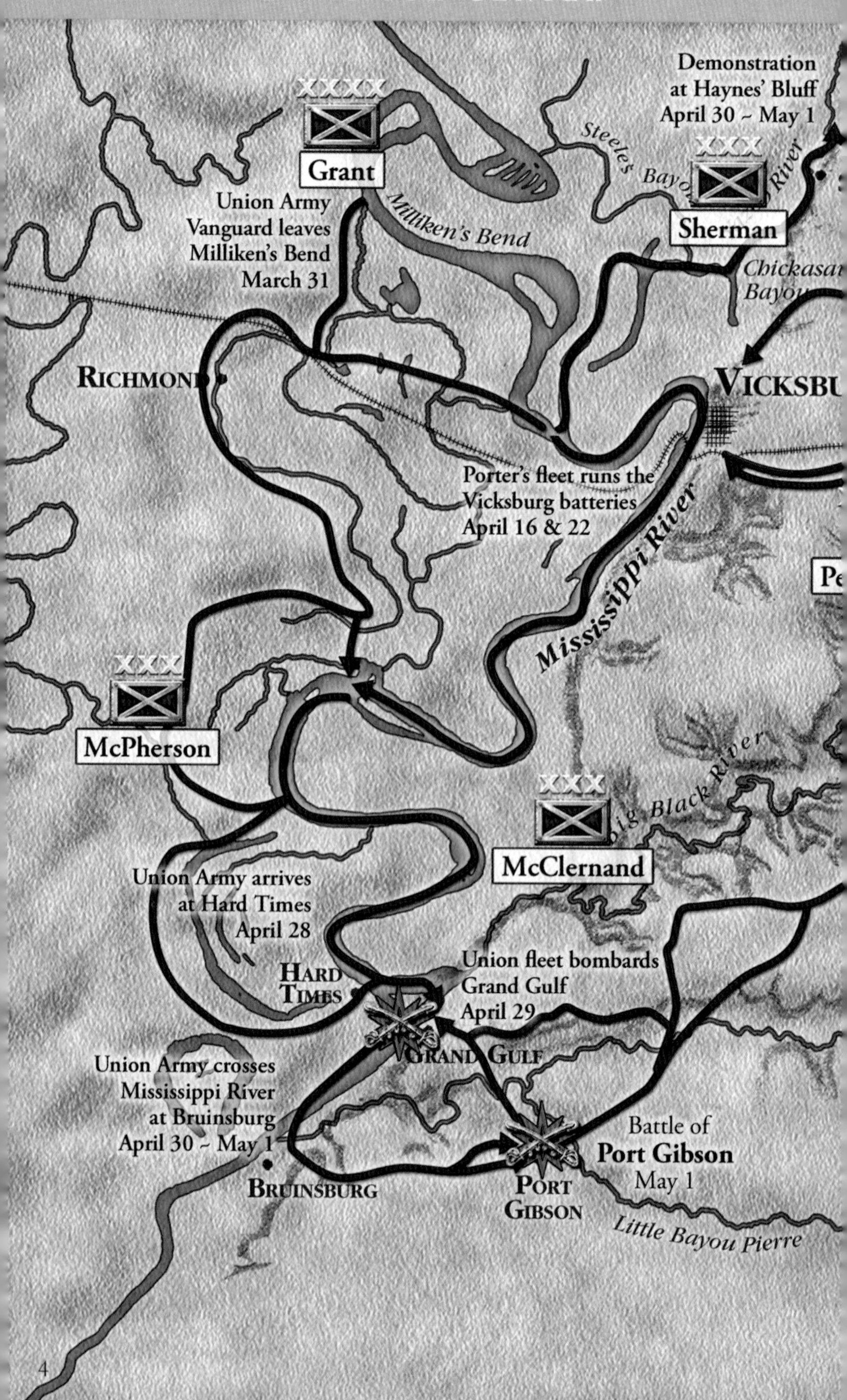
Demonstration
at Haynes' Bluff
April 30 ~ May 1
Grant
Sherman
Steeles Bayou
Union Army
Vanguard leaves
Milliken's Bend
March 31
Milliken's Bend
Chickasaw
Bayou
RICHMOND
VICKSBU
Porter's fleet runs the
Vicksburg batteries
April 16 & 22
Mississippi River
McPherson
McClernand
Big Black River
Union Army arrives
at Hard Times
April 28
HARD
TIMES
Union fleet bombards
Grand Gulf
April 29
GRAND GULF
Union Army crosses
Mississippi River
at Bruinsburg
April 30 ~ May 1
BRUINSBURG
Battle of
Port Gibson
May 1
PORT
GIBSON
Little Bayou Pierre

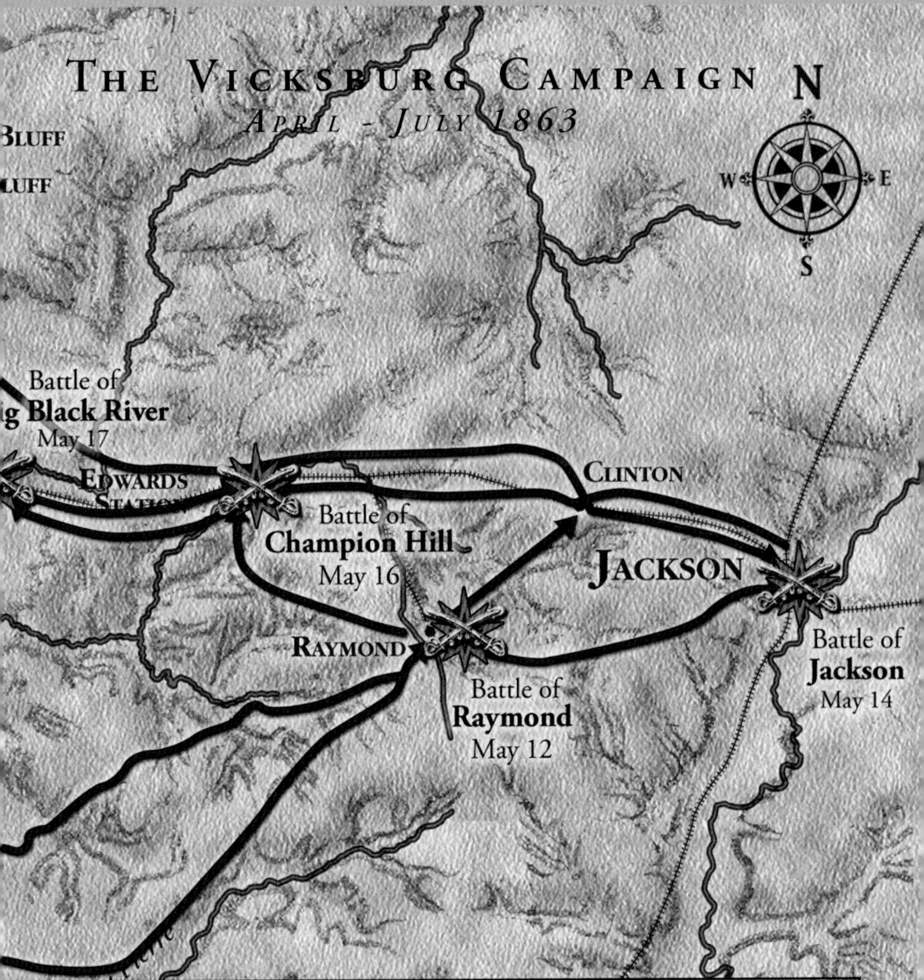

The Vicksburg Campaign

April - July 1863

N
W E
S

Bluff
luff

Battle of
g Black River
May 17

Edwards
Statio

Battle of
Champion Hill
May 16

Clinton

Jackson

Raymond

Battle of
Raymond
May 12

Battle of
Jackson
May 14

On May 16, 1863, Grant's Army of the Tennessee decisively defeated Pemberton's Army of Vicksburg at the Battle of Champion Hill.

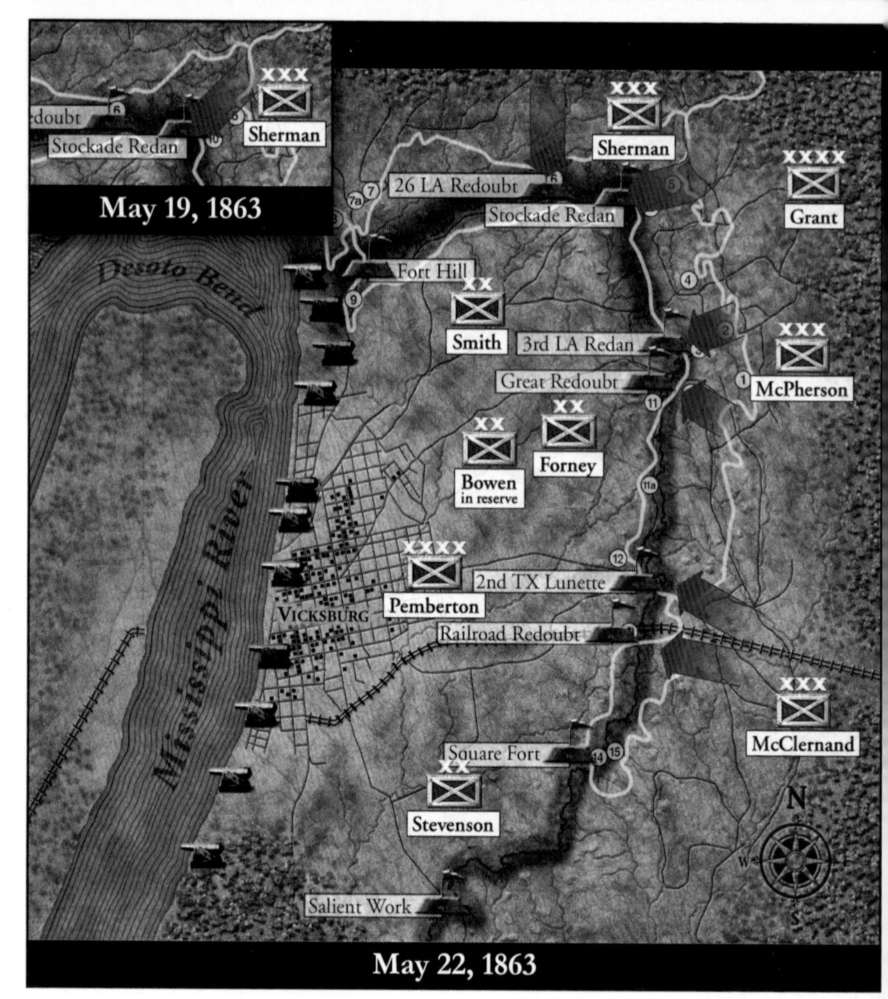

Assaults on Fortress Vicksburg: May 19 & 22, 1863

Following the Union victory at Big Black River on May 17th, the Confederates withdrew to the safety of Vicksburg. Despite the city's formidable defenses, Grant hoped to avoid a long and costly siege by attacking as soon as possible. On the morning of May 19, 1863, Grant gave orders for an assault to commence at 2:00 p.m. Unfortunately, when the signal to advance was sounded, only Sherman's troops were in position to attack. The men advanced under a heavy fire and were forced to withdraw before they could breach the Confederate works.

Undaunted, Grant ordered another attack on May 22, 1863. This time all three Union corps advanced on a broad front against the Confederate works. To the north, Sherman attacked the Stockade Redan. In the middle, McPherson attacked the Confederate works around the 3rd LA Redan and Great Redoubt. To the south, McClernand attacked the Railroad Redoubt. As the afternoon wore on, Grant was ready to call off the attack when a message from McClernand arrived that slightly exaggerated his gains and called for a renewed attack all along the line. Grant was skeptical, but ordered the attacks. The end result was further losses of Union troops. Grant eventually called off the attacks and resolved to take Vicksburg by siege.

Army of the Tennessee

Approximately 40,000 men

Grant
Commander

XIII Corps

McClernand

XV Corps

Sherman

XVII Corps

McPherson

XVI Corps

Hurlbut

Note: The XVI Corps was stationed in Memphis during campaign and assaults on Vicksburg.

Army of Vicksburg

Approximately 30,000 men

Pemberton
Commander

Bowen's Division

Bowen

Forney's Division

Forney

Loring's Division

Loring

Stevenson's Division

Stevenson

River Defense Forces

Smith's Division

Higgins

Smith

Note: Confederate commands were usually named after their commanders.

Gen. William Loring

Did you know?

Following the battle of Champion Hill on May 16, 1863, Loring and his division became separated from Pemberton's army. Rather than fight his way back to Vicksburg, Loring made a night march east to eventually join up with General Johnston. Loring was a colorful and controversial leader known for his short temper and excitable nature. Early in the war he had earned Robert E. Lee's enmity when he ordered a dangerous reconnaissance mission that cost the life of Lee's brother-in-law. Following the Civil War, Loring served in Egypt as a military advisor to the Khedive Ismail in 1869. Volatile as ever, Loring was involved in an altercation with the American Consul General that ended with shots being exchanged and the wounding of one of Loring's companions.

Military Symbols

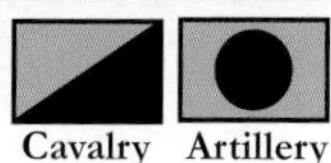

Infantry Cavalry Artillery

Army Organization

XXXX

Army

XXX

Corps

XX

Division

X

Brigade

III

Regiment

These symbols are used on the battlefield maps in this book to denote the general locations of troops.

Elements of a Siege

REDAN

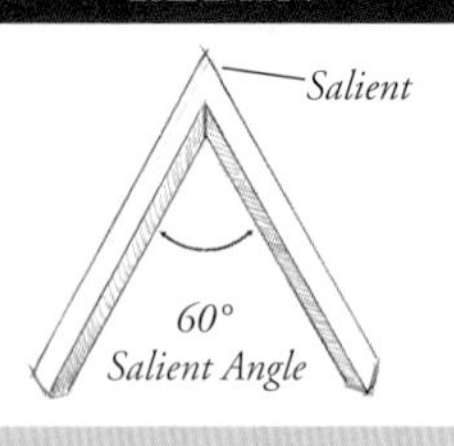

A fortification with two walls or parapets that met at a point called the salient. Because the Redan projected out from the line of defense, troops mounted along the walls could fire into the flanks of attacking enemy formations.

LUNETTE

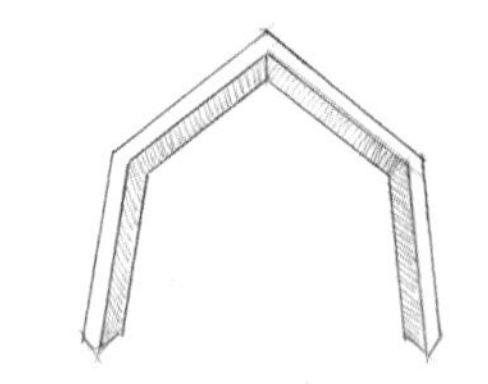

A redan with two base walls attached to extend the fortification out away from the main line. This extension allowed troops along its wall a better chance to fire into the attacker's flanks or rear.

REDOUBT

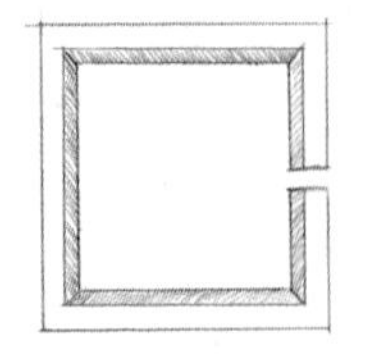

A detached earthwork that gave protection to its defenders from any direction of attack. Even if the line of fortified positions was broken, the garrison in a redoubt could fight on and act as a point of resistance.

Saproller – a man-made barrier, usually made out of hammered cane, that was placed at the head of the sap trench to protect the soldiers digging behind it. It was rolled forward as the trench advanced. At Vicksburg, Union soldiers in front of the 3rd Louisiana Redan improvised a saproller by piling cotton bales onto an old railroad cart.

Saps – a deep zigzagging trench that provided cover to soldiers as they approached the enemy's fortifications. During the siege, the Federals initiated thirteen major approaches to the Confederate defenses.

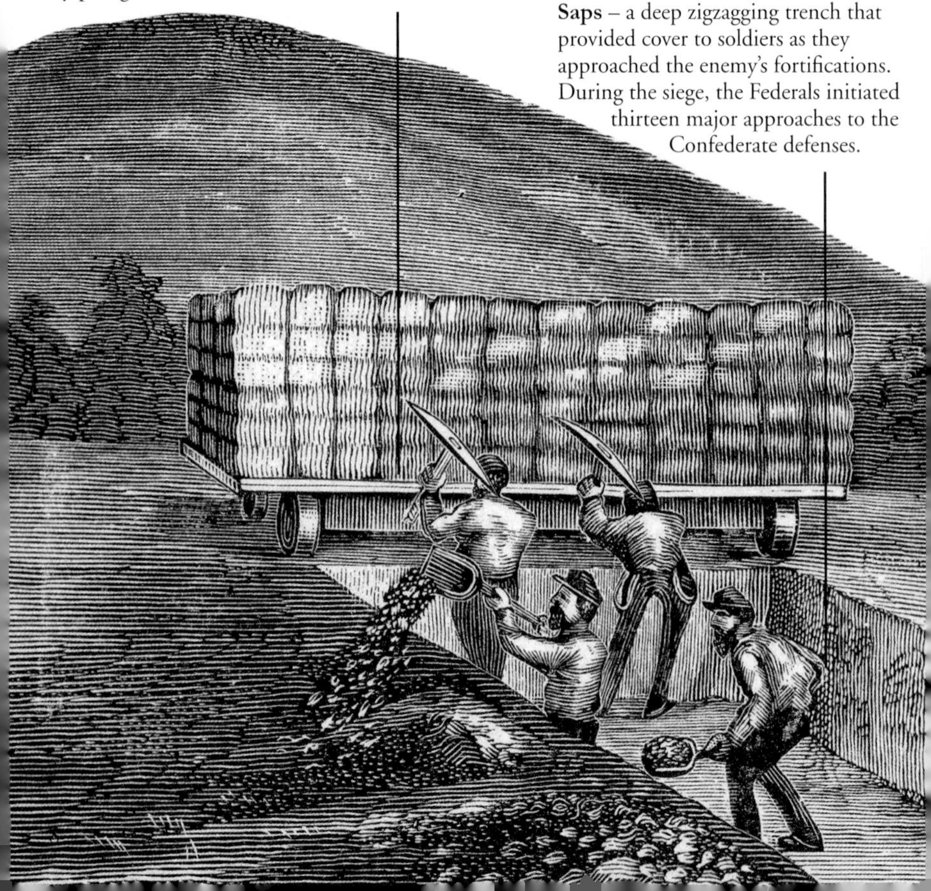

Capt. Samuel DeGolyer

Abatis (ăb′ə-tē,-tĭs) – A primitive form of barbed wire, abatis typically consisted of felled trees with their tops pointing towards the enemy and sawed-off limbs with sharpened points.

The Confederate earthworks at Vicksburg consisted of two major elements: the parapet and the ditch. The parapet is a protective mound of earth used to shelter the defender as well as provide an elevated position from which to fire. The ditch in front of the parapet functioned both as an obstacle and a source of earth for the parapet.

Gabions

Made of wicker and filled with dirt, gabions were used to strengthen walls in fortifications, battery positions and sap trenches. The sketch below depicts Union soldiers constructing gabions.

TravelBrains Trivia

Q1: Confederate army commander, John Pemberton, hailed from which state?

A. South Carolina

B. Virginia

C. Pennsylvania

Vicksburg resident, James Shirley, owned a house caught in the middle of the siege. Union soldiers called it the "White House" and dug a honeycomb of shelters all around it. The Shirley's were Union sympathizers. Their daughter Alice would later marry a Federal officer.

James Shirley

Alice Shirley

The Union troops in the vicinity of the Shirley House were often the target of a 20-pounder Parrott gun known as "Crazy Jane." In mid-June it was placed on the Confederate line near the Stockade Redan. Shortly thereafter, a shell from a Union gun tore off the last 9-inches of the Crazy Jane's muzzle. From that time on, the fire from the gun was highly erratic. Despite this, Confederate gunners would fire from 5 to 30 shots a day, doing great damage to the Union shanties dug all around the Shirley House.

This panorama was taken of the battlefield in the early twentieth century. Although over 40 years had passed since the time of the battle, the terrain was still much more open than it is today.

Pvt. Albert D.J. Cashire (right)

It is believed that as many as four hundred women served in the ranks of both the North and the South during the Civil War, disguised as men. At Vicksburg, a woman by the name of Jennie Hodges served with the 95th Illinois under the pseudonym, Albert D.J. Cashire. Private Cashire participated in approximately forty battles and skirmishes before her unit was mustered out of service at the end of the war. Her true identity remained undetected until nearly fifty years after the Vicksburg Campaign. In 1911 she was struck by an automobile and the surgeon who attended to her made the discovery. The war time photograph depicts Private Cashire sitting on the right. The inset picture is of Albert D.J. Cashire later in life.

Federal entrenchments in front of the 3rd LA Redan. On the horizon is Coonskin's Tower: a perch for Union sharpshooters.

Frederick Grant

Frederick Dent Grant was born on May 30, 1850, in St. Louis, Missouri, while his father was still serving in the old army. As a young boy during the Civil War he campaigned with his father, serving as his aide. After the war he attended West Point and graduated with the class of 1871. Assigned to the cavalry, he accompanied General Stanley in 1873 on the Yellowstone Expedition and one year later served with Custer during the Black Hills Expedition. In 1881 Grant resigned from the army to pursue business opportunities in New York. He later served as U.S. Minister to Austria and then as a New York Police Commissioner before returning to active duty in the army, when the Spanish American War broke out in 1898. At the beginning of the war Grant was stationed in Puerto Rico. Later he commanded troops in the Philippines. He would serve the rest of his life in the army, rising to the rank of major general. Frederick Grant died in New York City on April 12, 1912.

Illinois Memorial

Dedicated on October 26, 1906, the Illinois Memorial was modeled after the Roman Pantheon. Sixty bronze tablets line the interior walls displaying the names of 36,325 Illinois soldiers who participated in the Vicksburg Campaign. Around the exterior of the monument are the words of Lincoln's immortal second inaugural address, "With malice toward none, let us have peace."

FAMILY ACTIVITY

Find the names of Frederick Grant and Albert D. J. Cashire on the bronze plaques inside the monument. Frederick (shortened to Fred'k on the plaque) is located with the Army of the Tennessee staff and Pvt. Cashire can be found on the 95 IL, Co. G plaque.

FRED'K D. GRANT, AID | CASHIRE, ALBERT D. J.

One-ton bronze eagle, gilded in gold leaf

47 steps lead to the entrance, one for each day of the Siege of Vicksburg

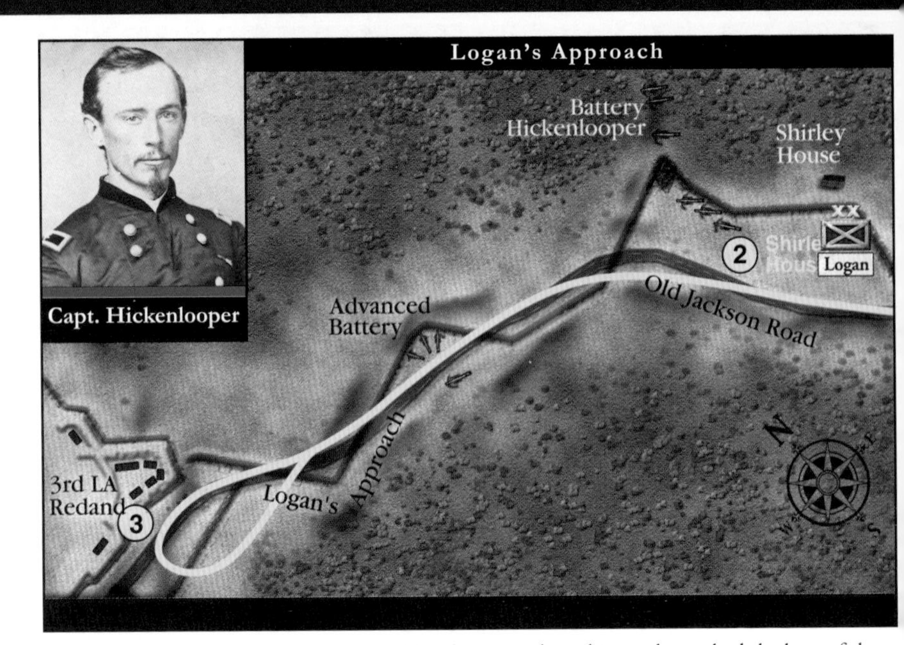

Logan's Approach zigzagged along the Old Jackson Road until it nearly reached the base of the 3rd Louisiana Redan. The Federals then dug a mine that extended forty feet under the redan and packed it with 2,200 pounds of black powder.

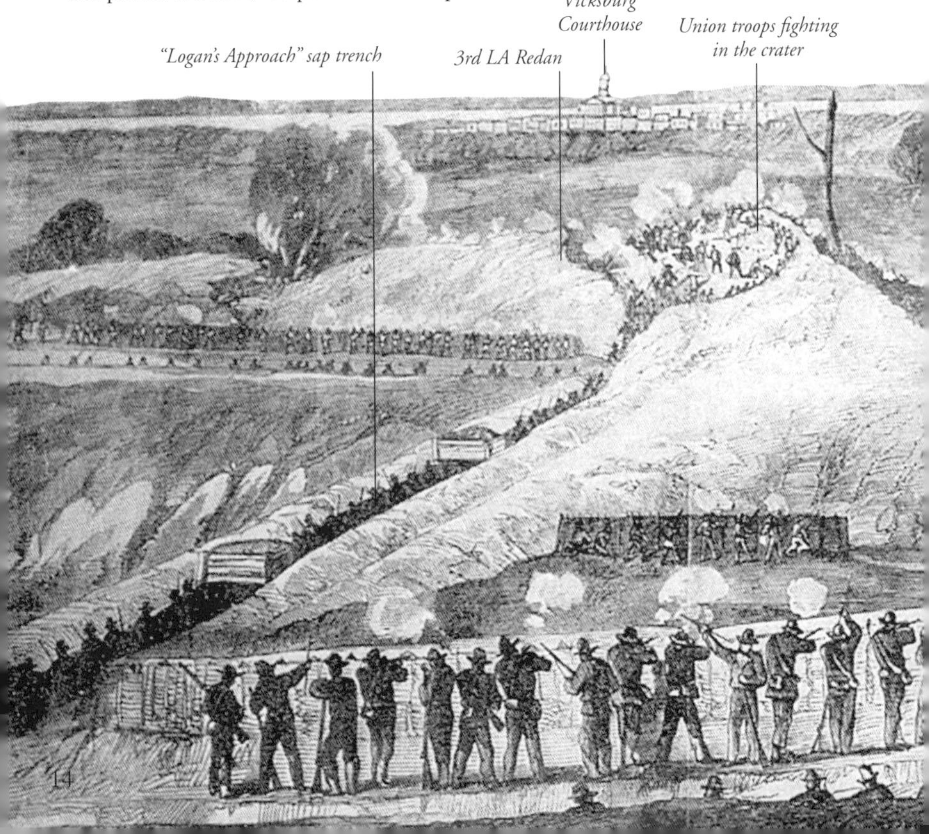

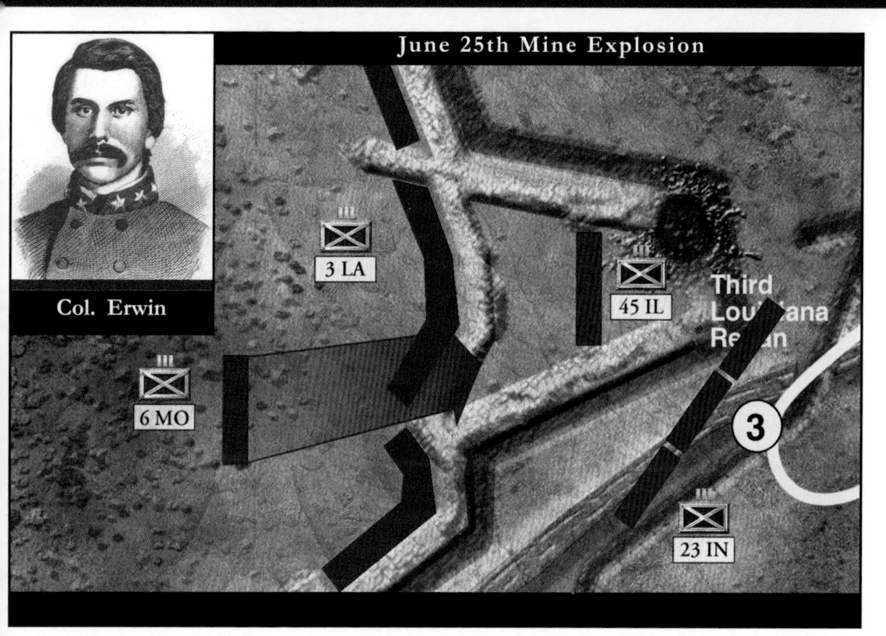

Col. Erwin

At 3:30 p.m. on June 25, the mine was detonated. The enormous explosion left a hole forty feet wide and 12 feet deep. The 45th Illinois charged into the crater, but was stopped almost immediately by a hail of musket fire. Confederate colonel Eugene Erwin was shot down leading the 6th Missouri in an attempt to drive the Federals out of the crater. After several unsuccessful attempts to breach the Confederate defense, the Federals withdrew and began a second mine.

Union view of the fighting in the crater on June 25, 1863

Col. Jasper Maltby

The regimental flag of the 45th Illinois

The commander of the 45th Illinois was Colonel Jasper A. Maltby. Prior to the Civil War, Maltby had established a gunsmith business in Galena, Illinois. By the end of the war, Maltby would be one of nine generals who had made Galena their home at some point during their pre-war lives, Ulysses S. Grant being the most famous. Severely wounded during the fighting in the redan crater on June 25, 1863, Maltby survived his wounds and was promoted to Brigadier General in August 1863. After the war, he was appointed Mayor of Vicksburg. He died while in office, serving the city he fought so hard to subdue.

TravelBrains Trivia

Q2: What was the "Widow Blakely?"

A. Famous cannon

B. Vicksburg civilian

C. Ironclad gunboat

Abraham

When the first mine exploded under the 3rd Louisiana Redan, a black slave known as Abraham was literally blasted to freedom. He had been working in the redan when the explosion threw him and the surrounding earth high into the air. Remarkably, he survived the fall and landed inside the Union lines. Abraham became something of a celebrity and went into service with the U.S. Quartermaster Department.

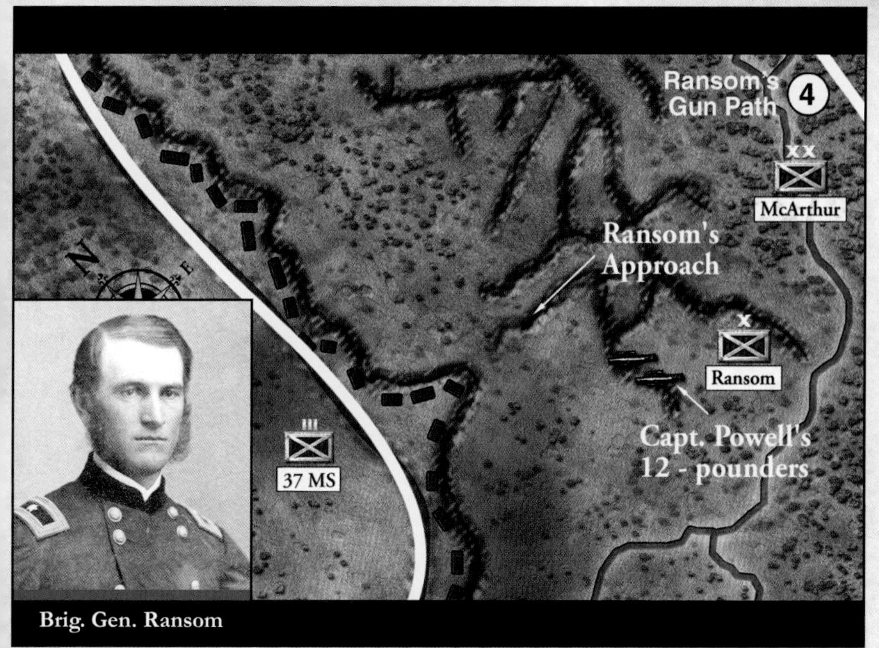

Brig. Gen. Ransom

Capt. Perkins

OLD ABE was the eagle mascot of the 8th Wisconsin. Captain John Perkins of Company C named the bird in honor of President Abraham Lincoln. During battles, Old Abe accompanied the men into action while tethered to his perch (pictured below). Old Abe survived the war and ended up living in the Wisconsin state capitol. Today, Old Abe is immortalized on the insignia patch of the 101st Airborne "Screaming Eagles."

Insignia patch of the 101st Airborne "Screaming Eagles"

Artillery of the Civil War

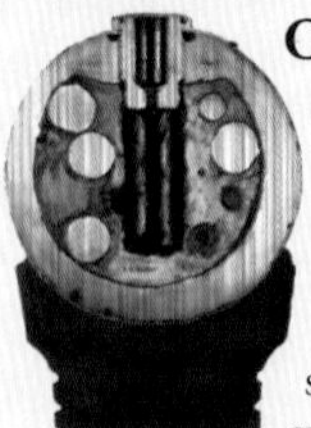

Case Shot

Case shot, sometimes called shrapnel, was a hollow iron shell (round or elongated) filled with round balls and sealed in melted rosin or sulphur. A powder charge in the core of the shell was ignited by a timed fuse. When the shell exploded, the balls and twisted fragments of iron tore through soldiers and horses.

Shell

A shell was a cast iron projectile (round or elongated) filled with black powder. Artillerists could choose an impact fuse or time fuse to explode the shell. An impact fuse exploded when it hit a target. A time fuse was ignited by the discharge of the cannon and exploded at a set time after ignition. Experienced artillerists could accurately time the fuse to explode the shell over the target.

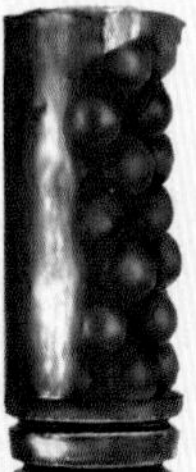

Canister

Canister was a tin can filled with iron balls (a little smaller than the size of golf balls) packed in sawdust. This type of ammunition effectively turned the cannon into a large shotgun. It was used at close range against infantry. In extreme cases, double and triple canister rounds were packed into the cannon muzzle and fired.

Solid Shot

Solid Shot was a round ball or elongated projectile made of solid iron. It was typically used at longer ranges against massed troops, fortifications, and enemy batteries. Solid shot (or bolts as they were sometimes called when fired from rifled cannon) were not designed to explode.

The Artillery Crew

A well-drilled crew could load and fire a cannon about three times per minute. A gun crew of ten men was ideal. A lieutenant and a sergeant gave orders; a gunner aimed the cannon; and the remaining seven crew members, each identified with a number, cleaned, loaded and fired the cannon.

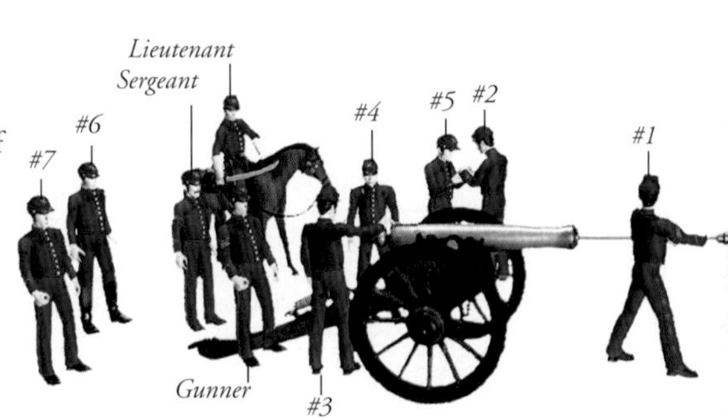

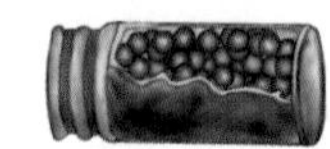

0 yds.

12-Pounder Napoleon

This famous cannon was named after Emperor Napoleon III of France. The term "12-Pounder" comes from the twelve-pound artillery round it fired. By the end of the Civil War it was by far the most widely used artillery piece in both armies. It had an effective range of one mile and could fire solid shot, shell, case shot and canister rounds. Made of bronze, the tube turns green as it oxidizes over time.

10-Pounder Parrott Rifle

This type of rifled cannon was made of cast iron with a wrought iron jacket and was named after Robert Parrott of the West Point Foundry. Cast iron guns were better at maintaining the rifle grooves on the inside of the tubes (bronze was too soft), but they were brittle and could crack or explode on discharge. Parrott devised a solution to this problem by wrapping a hot band of iron around the breech, or base, of the tube. You can easily identify Parrott guns by this distinguishing feature that gives them extra strength.

3-Inch Ordnance Rifle

Made entirely of wrought iron, the 3-inch ordnance rifle was expensive and time consuming to produce. Its durability and accuracy, however, made it a favorite among artillerists on both sides of the war. The name of the cannon is derived from the diameter of the gun's bore, a standard nomenclature practice for rifled cannon. Smoothbore cannon, on the other hand, are typically referenced by the weight of the solid shot they fire.

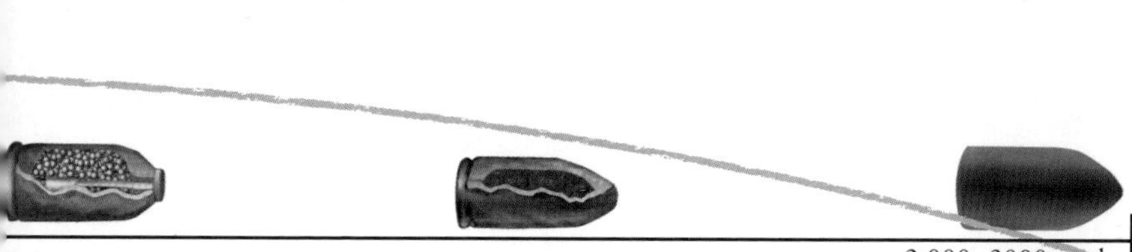

2,000- 3000 yards
Practical Range

CAPTAIN JOHN WESLEY POWELL, who had lost his right arm at the battle of Shiloh, commanded Company F, 2nd Illinois Artillery. With the help of Ransom's infantry, Powell and his men assembled two 12-pounder Napoleons in a position 100 yards from the enemy lines. While Ransom's men advanced the sap trench to within a few yards of the Confederate works, Powell and his Napoleons pounded away at the Rebels from close range.

Following the Civil War, Powell led the first successful expedition to navigate the mighty Colorado River. Lake Powell, created by damming part of the Colorado River, is named in his honor. Following his expedition, Powell headed the Smithsonian Institution's newly created Bureau of Ethnology. The bureau's mission was the collection and dissemination of information relevant to the Native American tribes. Also featured in the picture below are Wild Hank Sharp, Kentucky Mountain Bill, and Jesus Alviso.

TravelBrains Trivia

Q3: Which Union corps commander in the Army of the Tennessee was from Illinois?

A. McClernand

B. McPherson

C. Sherman

Q4: A well drilled Civil War artillery crew could fire how many rounds a minute?

A. 2

B. 3

C. 5

John Wesley Powell

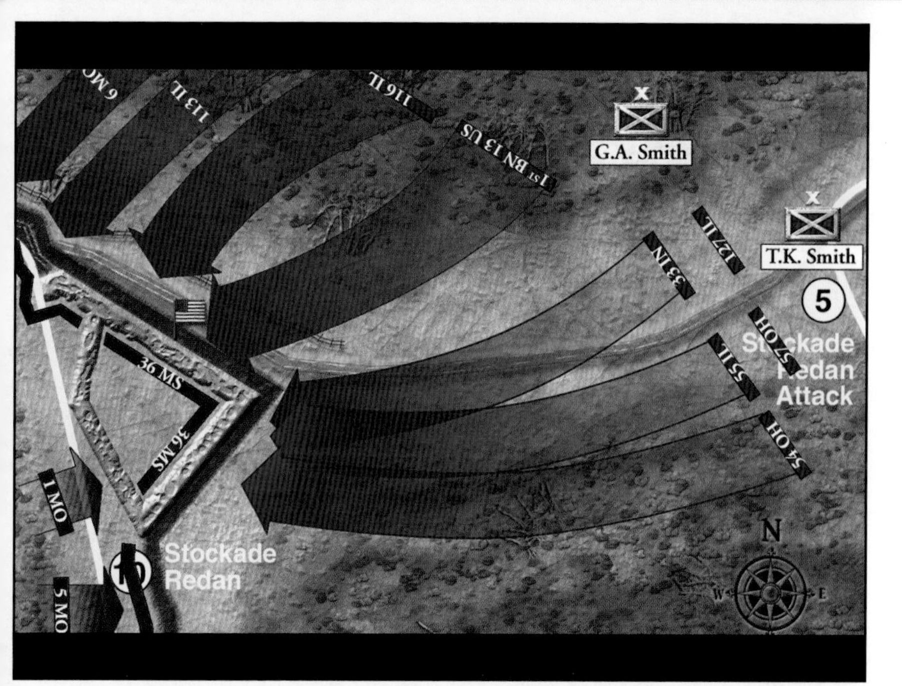

At 2:00 pm on May 19, 1863, the brigades of Union General Blair's division advanced against the Stockade Redan. Anticipating an attack in this sector, Pemberton drew from his reserves and sent elite regiments of Missourians from Cockrell's brigade forward to reinforce the walls just before the attack began. Although the 1st Battalion, 13th United States Infantry was able to reach the ditch and plant its colors on the slope of the Stockade Redan, it could not breach the Confederate defense. Sherman withdrew his battered units after nightfall.

Capt. Charles Ewing

Capt. Ewing was General Sherman's brother-in-law, as well as his foster brother.

Capt. Edward Washington was a grandnephew of George Washington.

Maj. Gen. William Tecumseh Sherman

William Tecumseh Sherman, like many other Civil War commanders, was a West Point graduate. He had served in the army through the end of the Mexican War and then resigned his commission. Later he accepted a position as president of Louisiana Military Seminary (now Louisiana State University) offered to him by two of his army friends, P.G.T. Beauregard and Braxton Bragg. When the Civil War broke out, Sherman went back north and accepted a commission as a colonel in the U.S. Army.

Orion P. Howe's fifes

Col. Oscar Malmborg & Orion P. Howe

The 55th Illinois infantry, the regiment to which Howe and Malmborg belonged, fought in 31 battles during the Civil War. During the war it received fewer than 50 replacements, while suffering 108 killed, 334 wounded and 49 men captured. It was one of the few regiments that fought in almost every battle of Sherman's military career, as well as, marched in every Confederate state, except for Texas and Florida.

Maj. Gen. Ulysses S. Grant

Ulysses S. Grant was born Hiram Ulysses Grant at Point Pleasant, Ohio, on April 27, 1822. During his enrolment at West Point a clerical error resulted in his name appearing as Ulysses Simpson Grant. Oddly enough, Grant found it easier to adopt the new version than to correct it. Later in life, some observers would quip that U.S. Grant stood for *Unconditional Surrender* Grant, a Nom de Guerre he earned following his demand for unconditional surrender at the Battle of Fort Donelson.

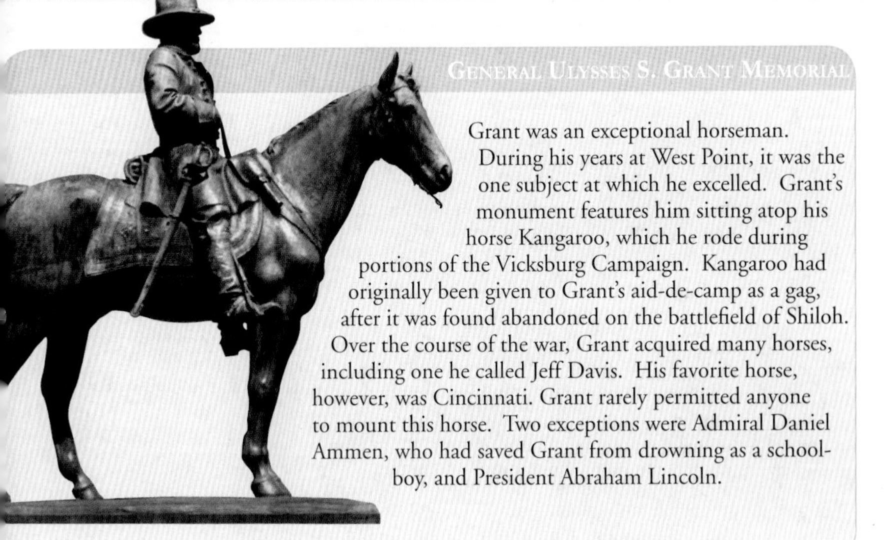

GENERAL ULYSSES S. GRANT MEMORIAL

Grant was an exceptional horseman. During his years at West Point, it was the one subject at which he excelled. Grant's monument features him sitting atop his horse Kangaroo, which he rode during portions of the Vicksburg Campaign. Kangaroo had originally been given to Grant's aid-de-camp as a gag, after it was found abandoned on the battlefield of Shiloh. Over the course of the war, Grant acquired many horses, including one he called Jeff Davis. His favorite horse, however, was Cincinnati. Grant rarely permitted anyone to mount this horse. Two exceptions were Admiral Daniel Ammen, who had saved Grant from drowning as a schoolboy, and President Abraham Lincoln.

Following his presidency, Grant fell on financially hard times and became ill with throat cancer. He worked tirelessly to complete his memoirs prior to his death, in order to leave his family a means of financial support.

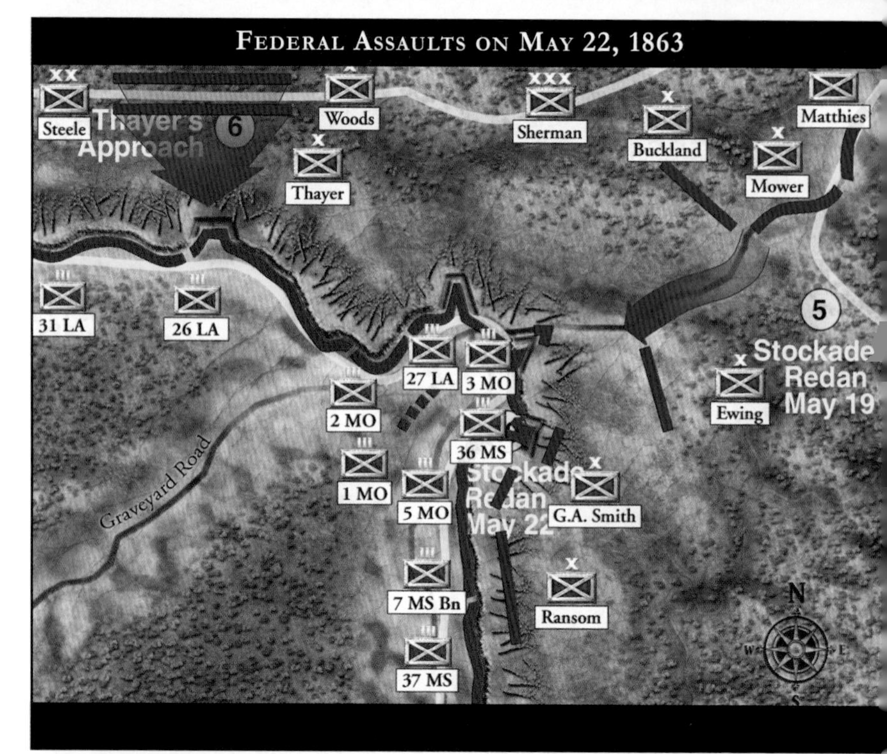

Brig. Gen. J. Thayer

Late in the afternoon of May 22, 1863, General Sherman ordered the attack resumed. Responding to the call, the brigades of Thayer and Woods attempted an assault on the 26th Louisiana Redoubt. Prior to the attack, Major Gustavus Lightfoot of the 12th Missouri pulled out a box of fine cigars and offered them to his fellow officers. When one of the men told him to save some of the cigars for later, Lightfoot responded, "Oh take them; I will have no further use for cigars; this is my last smoke!" His premonition would prove accurate. Lightfoot was killed in the assault up the steep slopes fronting the redan.

Maj. Gustavas Lightfoot monument

Col. C. Woods

Lt. Cmdr. Thomas O. Selfridge

The insignia that Lieutenant Commander Thomas Selfridge wore, while in command of the U.S.S. Cairo.

TravelBrains Trivia

Q5: Who is the city of Vicksburg named after?

A. Victor Hugo

B. Reverend Newit Vick

C. Queen Victoria

Q6: Which Union general was working as a clerk in his father's leather store in Galena, Illinois, when the Civil War started?

A. William T. Sherman

B. James McPherson

C. Ulysses S. Grant

On March 8, 1862, the Confederate ironclad C.S.S. Virginia rammed and sank the U.S.S. Cumberland at Hampton Roads, claiming the lives of two-thirds of her crew. Selfridge was a gunnery officer aboard the Cumberland and narrowly escaped. On December 12, 1862, Selfridge was commanding the U.S.S. Cairo when it struck an "infernal machine" (naval mine) and sank in the Yazoo River. Selfridge was next placed in command of the Conestoga, a timberclad gunboat. On March 8, 1864, exactly two years after the sinking of the Cumberland, the Conestoga collided with a steamer vessel and sank in about four minutes. "Thus for the third time in the war, I had my ship suddenly sunk under me," Selfridge wrote. "It is a strange coincidence that the names of these three ships all begin with the letter C," he added.

Sinking of the U.S.S. Cumberland

"Infernal Machines" (often called torpedoes during the Civil War) were essentially naval mines. These crude devices were inexpensive to produce and proved deadly. A wooden casket floated on top of the water and was attached to a submerged cylinder (often a five gallon glass jug) filled with gunpowder. An anchor kept it stationary and an insulated wire ran from the cylinder to the shore, where a soldier watched and waited. At the opportune moment, the soldier would hit a plunger on a galvanic cell (battery) and complete an electrical connection. The resulting current raced down the wire to the cylinder and exploded the mine.

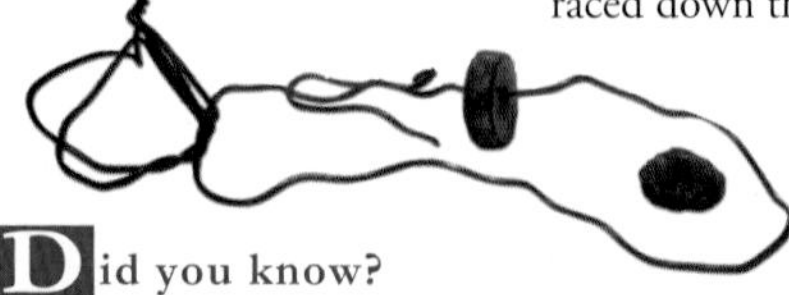

Fusewire, stopper and sealing wax from the mine that sank the U.S.S. Cairo (on display at the Old Courthouse Museum, Vicskburg)

Did you know?

David Glasgow Farragut was born James Glasgow Farragut near Knoxville Tennessee on June 6, 1801. He was later adopted by David Porter (David *Dixon* Porter's father) and trained to be a naval officer. Farragut eventually changed his first name from James to David in honor of his adopted father. Thus the famous Union admirals, David Glasgow Farragut and David Dixon Porter, are foster brothers.

Fleet Admirals

David Glasgow Farragut

In April 1862, while commanding the West Gulf Blockading Squadron, Farragut fought his way past two Confederate forts guarding the mouth of the Mississippi and captured New Orleans. The following month he proceeded upriver and bombarded Vicksburg, but was unable to silence the city's batteries. Farragut returned to New Orleans and quickly organized another expedition against Vicksburg. In late June his powerful flotilla passed the Vicksburg guns. Afraid that the river's receding water level would strand his ocean going vessels, he retired back to New Orleans.

Admiral Farragut

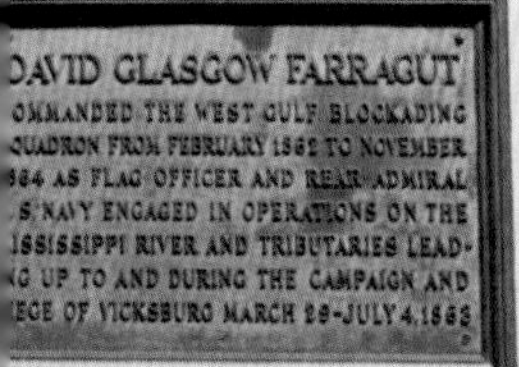

David Dixon Porter

Porter began the Civil War as a lieutenant and ended it as a vice admiral. In early 1862 he was the commander of the mortar flotilla attached to Farragut's squadron. After the capture of New Orleans, Porter assumed command of the Mississippi Squadron in October 1862. He worked closely with Grant during the Vicksburg campaign and ran past the guns of Vicksburg with his ironclads and transports on the nights of April 16 and 22, 1863. Porter ended the war commanding the North Atlantic Squadron.

Admiral Porter

Flag Officers

Andrew Hull Foote

Foote commanded a flotilla of gunboats on the upper Mississippi beginning in mid-1861. Working with General Grant, Foote oversaw the naval operations in the successful Union attacks on Forts Henry and Donelson. Later he also worked with Union General Pope in the capture of Island No. 10. Foote was wounded at Fort Donelson and the injury became so disabling that he was forced to relinquish command to Charles Henry Davis in May of 1862.

Admiral Foote

Impatient to rejoin the war, he pressed for a command and eventually was given the South Atlantic Blockading Squadron. Still recovering from his wound, Foote died en route to his new command in June, 1863.

Admiral Davis

Charles Henry Davis

On May 9, 1862, Davis replaced Foote as the commander of the Western Flotilla. The very next day he fought an indecisive engagement off Fort Pillow. On June 6, 1862, he destroyed the Confederate fleet at Memphis and occupied the city. Proceeding south he joined Farragut in the unsuccessful attack on Vicksburg. Davis spent the remainder of the war as the chief of the Bureau of Navigation.

Ed Bearss on the site where the Cairo was raised.

Artifacts on display in the Cairo Museum

The bell of the Cairo

A restored timepiece that belonged to one of the Cairo's crew

A boatswain's pipe

On December 12, 1862, the U.S.S. Cairo became the first armed warship to be sunk by a mine (called a 'torpedo' or 'infernal machine' at the time).

> *"...just as we were training on the battery we were struck by a torpedo, which exploded under our starboard bow, a few feet from the center and some 35 or 40 feet from the bow proper just under our provision store room, which crushed in the bottom of the boat so that the water rushed in like the roar of Niagara. In five minutes the Hold was full of water and the forward part of the gunboat was flooded...One of our heaviest bow guns had been dismounted by the force of the explosion injuring three men."*
>
> \- George Yost, Cairo crew member

The U.S.S. Cairo was an Ironclad River Gunboat of the City Class. It came equipped with thirteen guns, including three large 64-pounder Navy smoothbores.

U.S.S. Cairo

Although the action depicted in this Currier and Ives print of the Siege of Vicksburg is fictitious, it effectively portrays the commanding height of Fort Hill. The position was so formidable, in fact, that no Union attacks were ever made against it.

1863

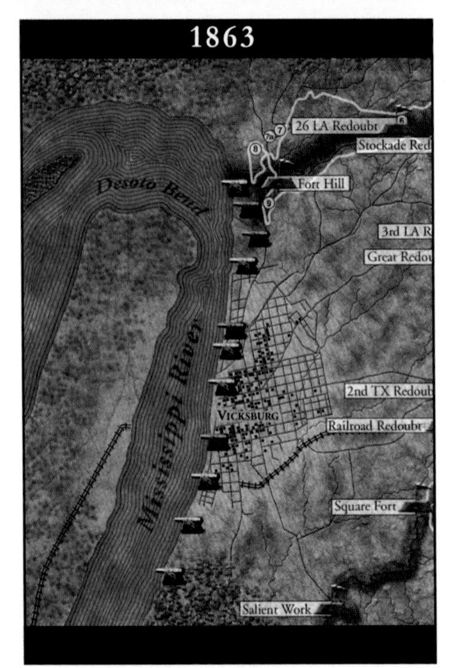

TODAY

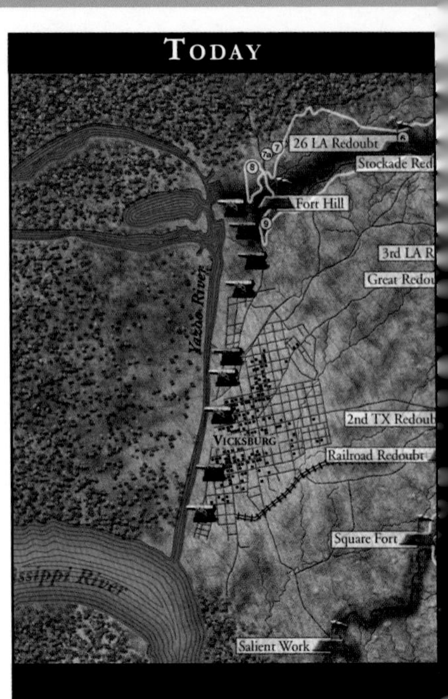

In 1876 nature accomplished what Grant could not pull off by force of will and the construction of a canal. It changed the course of the mighty Mississippi River. Suddenly Vicksburg was without a river front. In 1903 the Army Corps of Engineers diverted the Yazoo River to run past the city.

The photograph below shows one of the Confederate river batteries that made running the gauntlet of Vicksburg so dangerous for Porter's fleet. The photograph was taken after the surrender of the city. Union tents can be seen in the background.

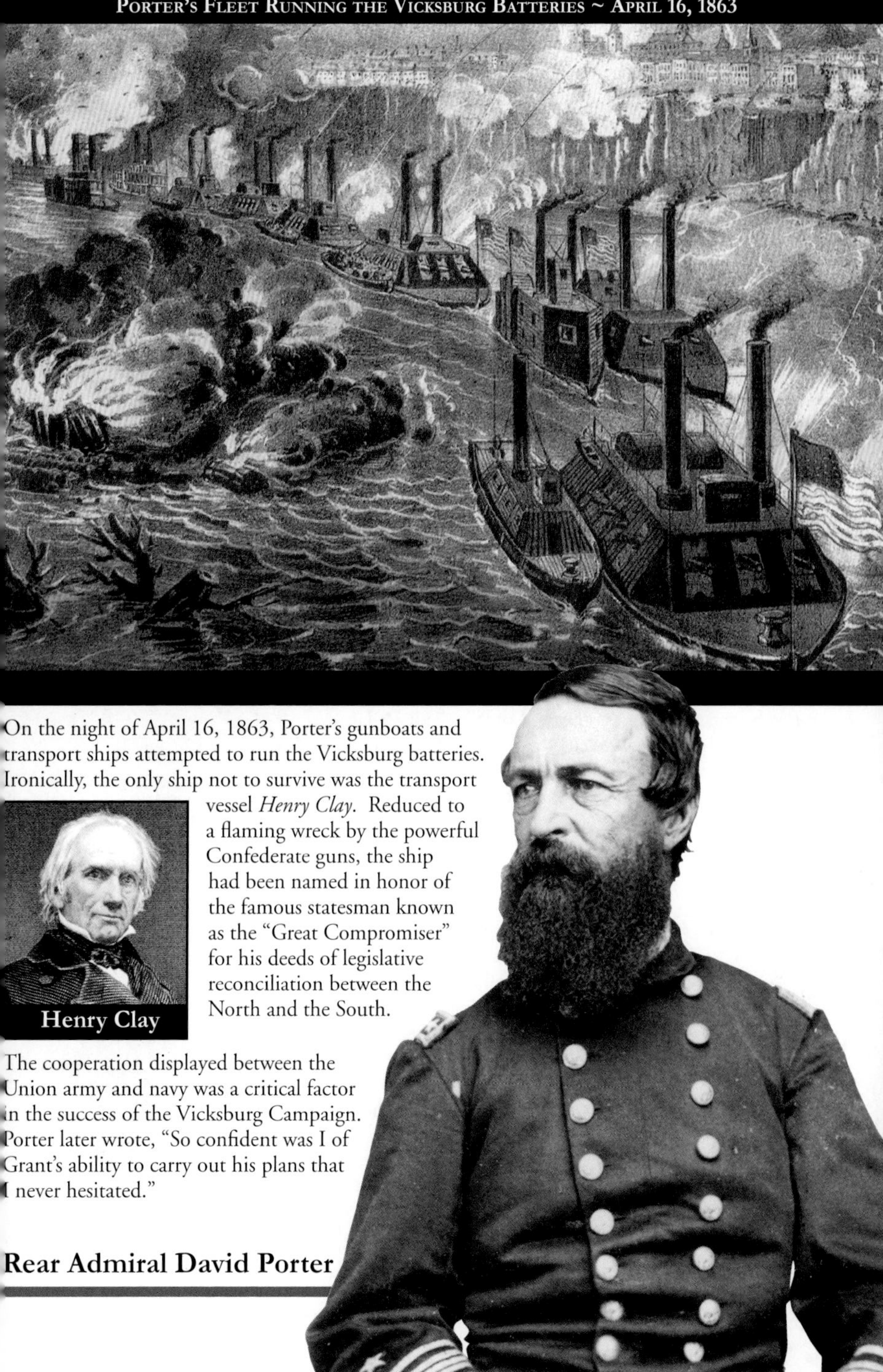

PORTER'S FLEET RUNNING THE VICKSBURG BATTERIES ~ APRIL 16, 1863

On the night of April 16, 1863, Porter's gunboats and transport ships attempted to run the Vicksburg batteries. Ironically, the only ship not to survive was the transport vessel *Henry Clay*. Reduced to a flaming wreck by the powerful Confederate guns, the ship had been named in honor of the famous statesman known as the "Great Compromiser" for his deeds of legislative reconciliation between the North and the South.

Henry Clay

The cooperation displayed between the Union army and navy was a critical factor in the success of the Vicksburg Campaign. Porter later wrote, "So confident was I of Grant's ability to carry out his plans that I never hesitated."

Rear Admiral David Porter

Capt. John H. Groce

At 10:00 am on the morning of May 22, 1863, Sherman sent a battering ram of men down the Graveyard Road. Leading the way were a 150 volunteers of the *Forlorn Hope*. Their job was to bridge the ditch that fronted the Stockade Redan. As they emerged from a cut in the road, a hail of Confederate musket fire cut them down. Only a handful of men reached the ditch and the attack soon bogged down.

The 30th Ohio Monument

Rather than construct a single state memorial, Ohio chose to construct a small monument for each of thirty-nine units that participated in the Vicksburg Campaign. This monument commemorates the officers and men of the 30th Ohio Volunteer Infantry Regiment. On the Morning of May 22, 1863, the 30th Ohio charged down the Graveyard Road behind the *Forlorn Hope*. A storm of Confederate musket fire brought it to a stop in the small cut that the road made through the ridge line. Only a handful of men reached the ditch fronting the Stockade Redan.

A Medal of Honor awarded to one of the survivors of the Forlorn Hope.

Late in the afternoon on May 22, 1863, Sherman ordered another attack on the Stockade Redan. The Confederates, however, had been firmly reinforced by Cockrell's Missourians. Once again a column of bluecoats was cut down as it approached along the Graveyard Road. Recognizing the futility of the assault, Sherman called off the attack.

Brig. Gen. Joseph Mower

Col. Francis Cockrell

A *Harper's Weekly* sketch of Union and Confederate troops tossing hand grenades made from artillery shells with short-cut fuses.

William F. Ketchum of Buffalo, New York, invented and patented a new type of hand grenade on August 20, 1861. Ketchum's innovative design involved a contact fuse made with a plunger and spring that fit into a hollow tube. The plunger would ignite a percussion cap surrounded by gun powder inside the hollow tube when the grenade struck the ground. Over 90,000 of these weapons were manufactured in 1, 3 and 5-pound sizes. Fins were attached to the rear of the grenade to make it more aerodynamic. The success rate in actual combat left something to be desired, however. Stories abound of Confederates catching the grenades in blankets and then hurling them back at their surprised Union opponents. This Ketchum Hand Grenade was found in the wreckage of the U.S.S. Cairo.

TravelBrains Trivia

Q7: During the siege of Vicksburg, which essential military tool was constantly in short supply for the Confederates?

A. Artillery shells

B. Gun powder

C. Percussion caps

Q8: Who was Ulysses S. Grant's best man at his wedding?

A. William T. Sherman

B. James Longstreet

C. J.E.B. Stuart

ARKANSAS STATE MEMORIAL

BROTHER VS BROTHER

Missouri was a border state during the Civil War. The citizens of the state were so divided over their loyalties that they formed two state governments, one pro-Union the other pro-Southern. They also supplied troops to both sides. At Vicksburg there were 27 Union and 15 Confederate units from the state of Missouri. The Missouri state memorial is located, in fact, where two opposing Missouri regiments fought each other.

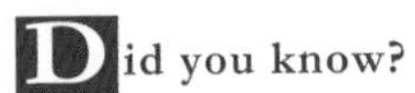

Civil War soldiers wore different brass insignia to identify the arm of service to which they belonged.

Infantry

Artillery

Cavalry

Missouri State Memorial

Dedicated to Missouri soldiers who fought for both the Union and Confederacy

Bronze statue of the "Spirit of the Republic" emerging from the war with new strength

Bronze plaque depicting Missouri Federals attacking this position

Bronze plaque depicting Missouri Confederates defending this position

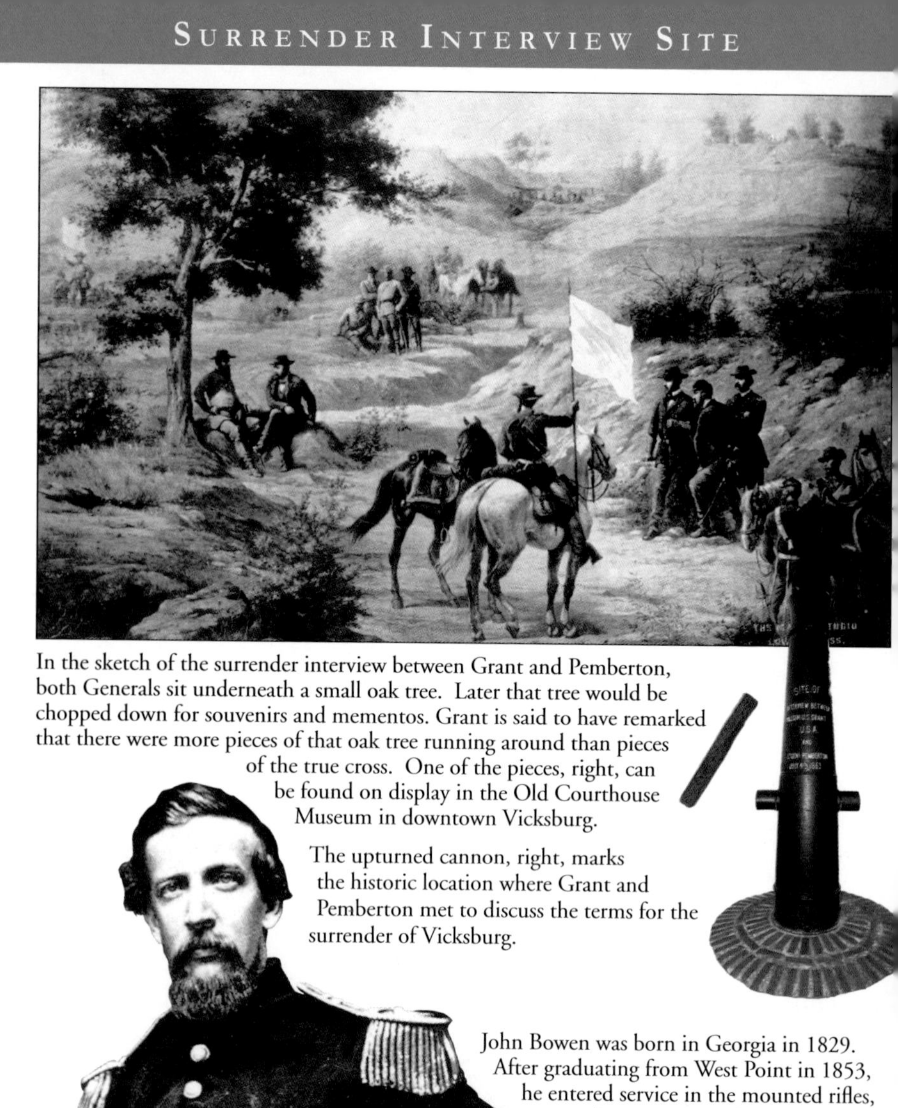

In the sketch of the surrender interview between Grant and Pemberton, both Generals sit underneath a small oak tree. Later that tree would be chopped down for souvenirs and mementos. Grant is said to have remarked that there were more pieces of that oak tree running around than pieces of the true cross. One of the pieces, right, can be found on display in the Old Courthouse Museum in downtown Vicksburg.

The upturned cannon, right, marks the historic location where Grant and Pemberton met to discuss the terms for the surrender of Vicksburg.

John Bowen was born in Georgia in 1829. After graduating from West Point in 1853, he entered service in the mounted rifles, spending a portion of his time on the Frontier. He resigned in 1856 to pursue a career as an architect, first in Savannah, Georgia, then in St. Louis Missouri.

Ulysses. S. Grant recognized Bowen, because the future president used to deliver firewood to residents of Bowen's town. During the Vicksburg surrender negotiations, General Bowen was suffering from dysentery. The disease took his life on July 13, 1863.

Maj. Gen. John S. Bowen

While the Federals laid siege to Vicksburg, General Joseph E. Johnston was assembling an army to relieve the embattled city. Unfortunately for Johnston, General Robert E. Lee was conducting the Gettysburg Campaign at the time, making it difficult to draw extra troops from the east.

By the time Johnston had pooled together a force of 31,000, Grant's army had swelled in size and was prepared to keep Vicksburg under siege while it fended off any attacks from the east. Johnston was not eager to attack. On June 15 he made his feelings know to his superiors, stating, "I consider saving Vicksburg hopeless."

On July 1, Johnston's army approached the east bank of the Big Black River, hoping to find a vulnerable spot in the Federal line. After three days of reconnaissance, the point was mute. Vicksburg surrendered on July 4, 1863.

Following the Civil War, Johnston served in Congress and died in 1891, after catching a cold attending the funeral of his former adversary, William Tecumseh Sherman.

Gen. Joseph E. Johnston

This sketch depicts Union troops parading into Vicksburg. In the background is the historic Old Court House, a prominent Vicksburg landmark.

Painting of the 4th Minnesota marching into Vicksburg.

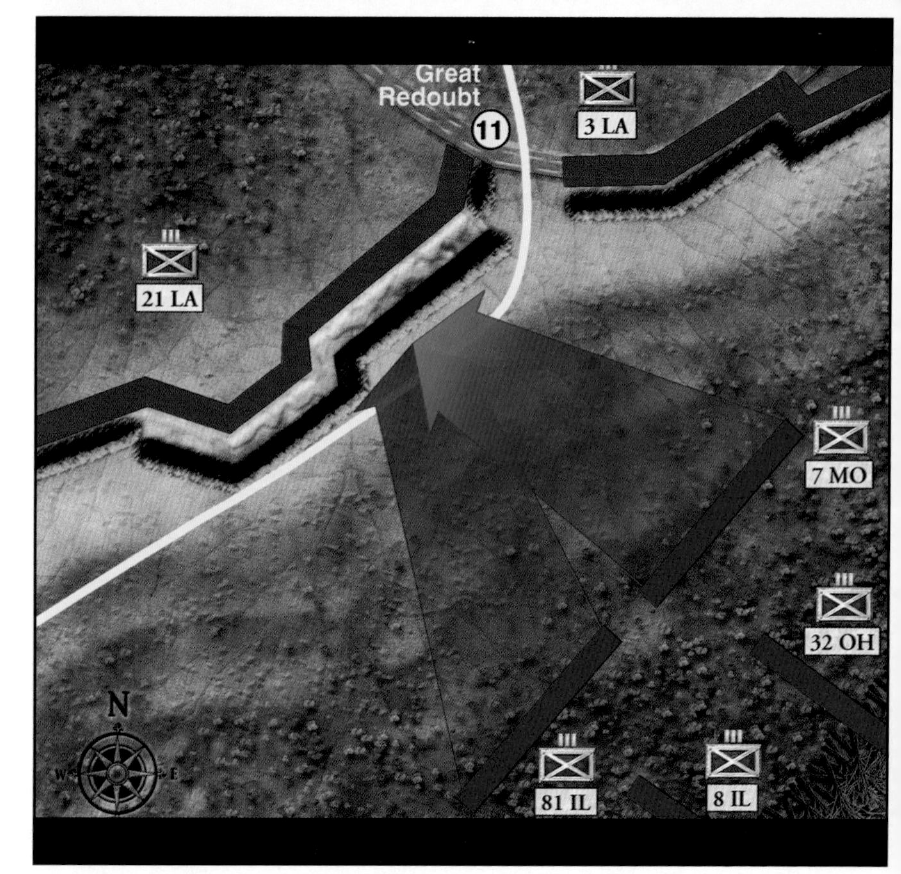

At 10:00 am on May 22, Union General John Stevenson led his brigade forward against the Great Redoubt. In front was the mostly Irish 7th Missouri with their emerald battle flag waving in the air. When the Missourians reached the walls of the Great Redoubt they discovered that their scaling ladders were too short to reach the top of the Confederate parapet.

A *Harper's Weekly* sketch of Capt. Stewart R. Tresilian's tree trunk mortars.

The 7th Missouri flag. Embroidered on it were the words "Erin Go Bragh", meaning "Ireland Forever."

Did you know?

The Minié Ball was named after French army officer Claude-Etienne Minié. Upon firing, the hollow base of the bullet would expand in the barrel forcing it against the rifle grooves that lined the tube. As a result, the bullet would spiral out of the barrel and achieve greater accuracy and range.

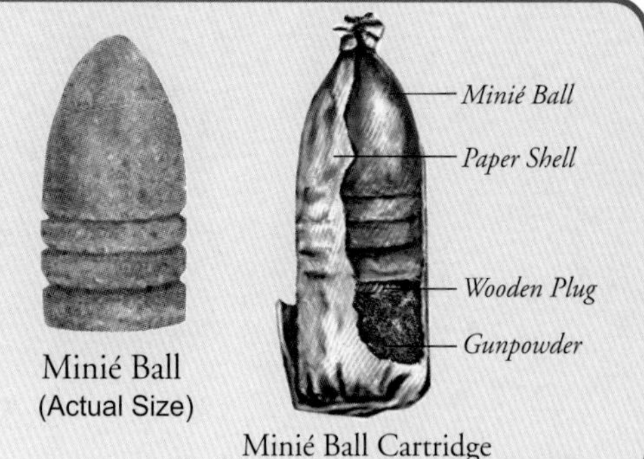

Minié Ball
(Actual Size)

Minié Ball Cartridge

Panorama of the Great Redoubt in the early 1900s

Lt. Gen. John C. Pemberton

When Pemberton surrendered Vicksburg, 709 Confederates refused to sign paroles, preferring instead to go to Union prison camps.

Mrs. Pemberton

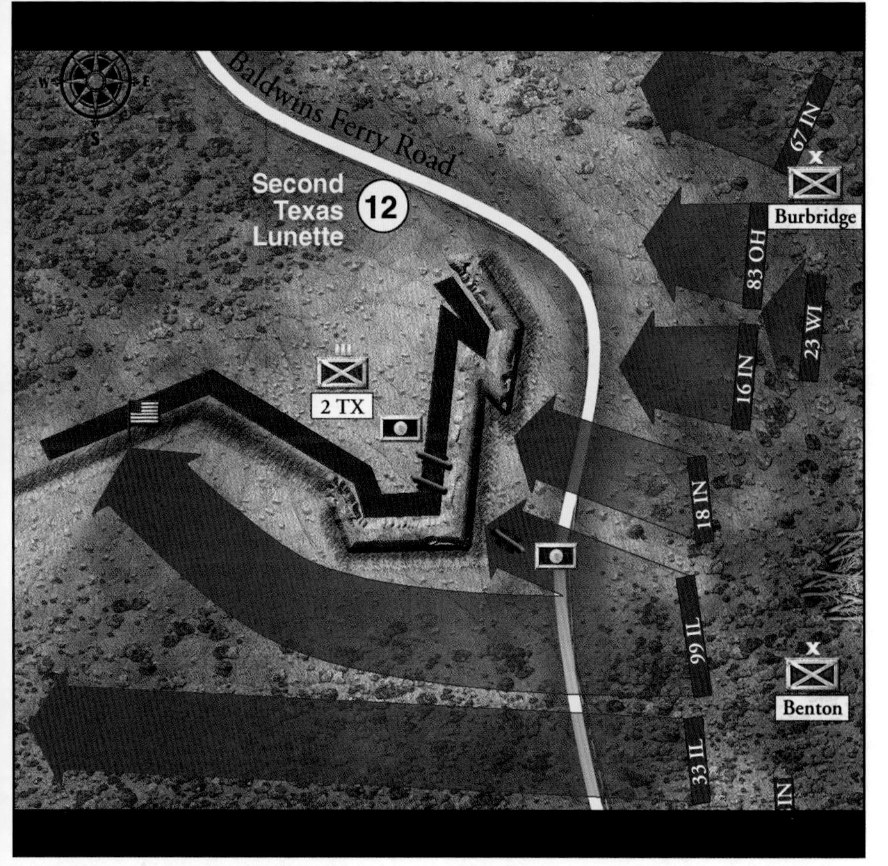

At 10:00 am on May 22, 1863, the Union brigades of Burbridge and Benton assaulted the 2nd Texas Lunette. Although they reached the ditch fronting the lunette, they could not force their way inside.

Brig. Gen. Moore

Brig. Gen. Benton

Brig. Gen. Burbridge

Jefferson Davis Monument

Cpl. Thomas J. Higgins

The national colors carried at one time by the 99th Illinois. It is uncertain whether it was the flag carried by Higgins at Vicksburg.

Capt. Patrick White

Patrick White's Sword

This sword was lost when Capt. White was captured by Confederates in the Spring of 1864, during the disastrous Red River Campaign of General Nathaniel Banks. White spent the remainder of the war in a Confederate prison camp. For over 27 years the sword hung above the mantel of Alex McDow, the Confederate officer who had captured White. Some years after McDow's death in 1891, his daughter began running a small advertisement in a Union veterans magazine offering to return the sword to Captain White. It wasn't until 1899 that White, by chance, noticed the tiny ad and was reunited with his lost sword after 35 years. White died in Albany, New York, on November 25, 1915.

A 6-pounder cannon of the type that Captain White dragged to the edge of the 2nd Texas Lunette

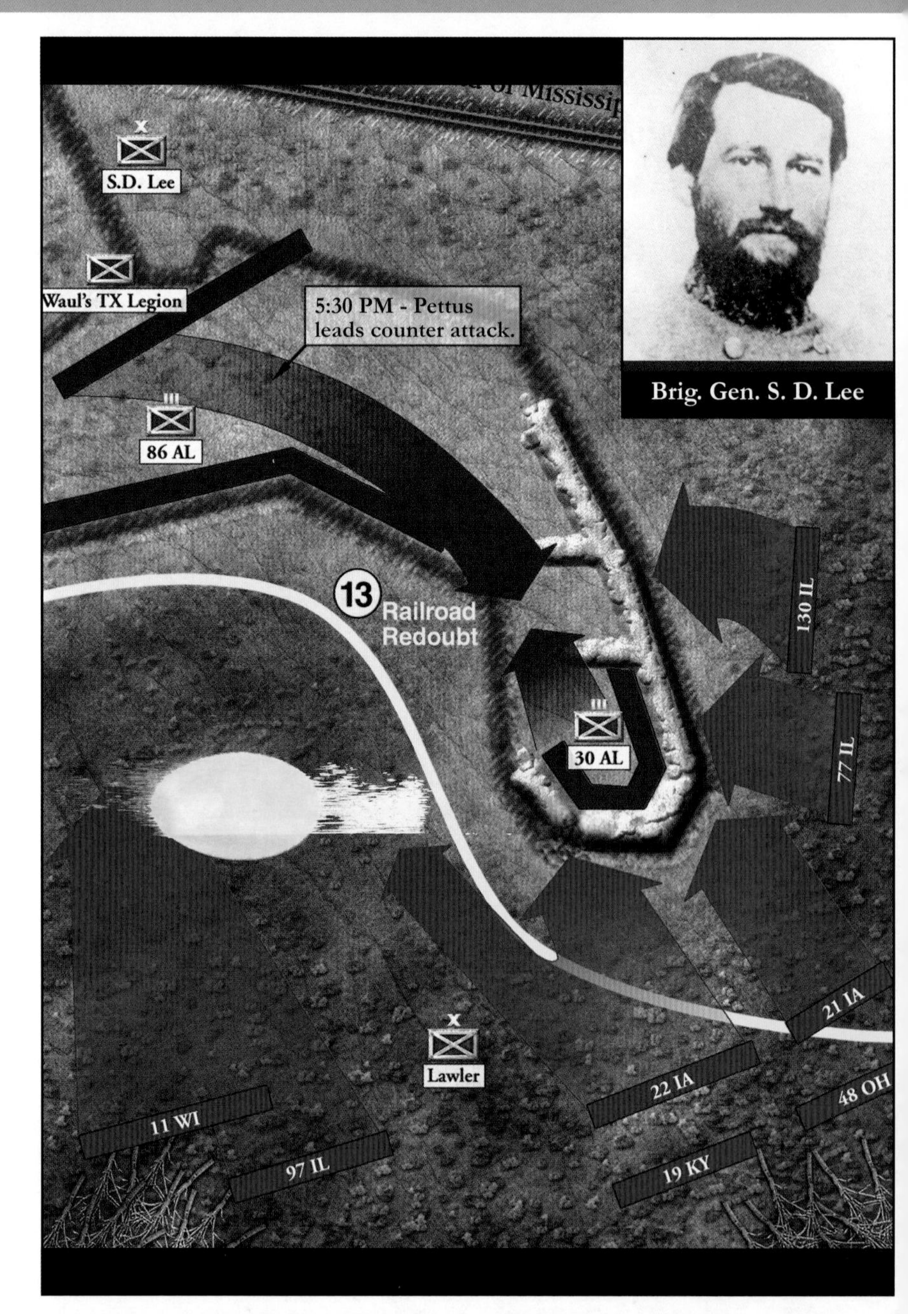

Brig. Gen. S. D. Lee

At 10:00 am on May 22, 1863, the Union brigades of Lawler and Landram swept forward to assault the Railroad Redoubt. After the tip of the redoubt had been battered down by Union artillery, the men from the 22nd Iowa were able to battle their way inside. Fighting raged all day for possession of the redoubt, until a spirited Confederate counterattack led by Col. Edmund Pettus drove the Union troops out of the redoubt and back into the ditch and then away from the redoubt.

Brig. Gen. Michael K. Lawler

Sgt. J. E. Griffith

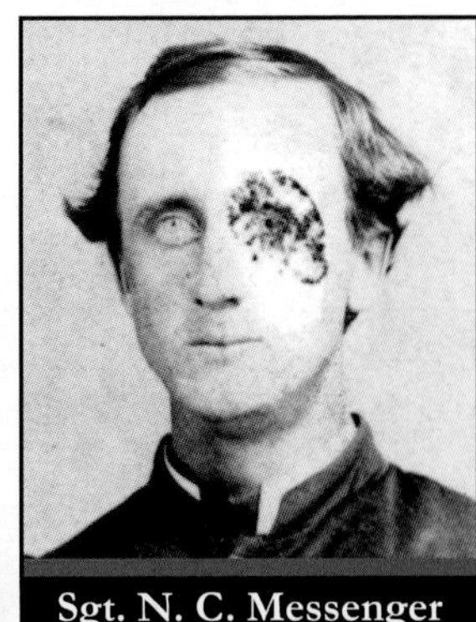

Sgt. N. C. Messenger

"About 10:15, our army arose at once as if by magic out of the ground. *Then commenced the ordeal. The regiment on a charge started for the fort. At once the Confederates opened with grape and canister, plowing gaps through our ranks. Steadily, we pushed on up the slope into the ditch and over the parapet, placed the flag on the fort, and kept it there for some time. Thirteen prisoners were taken out of the fort, only a few of our boys got into the fort and they had to come out of it, and remained in the ditch outside. By this time the Confederates that fled or were driven away returned with re-enforcements, so we now had to protect ourselves the best we could... The rebels for a moment stood on the top of their rifle pits, pouring the deadly shot into us. Then was our sharpshooter's opportunity, and well they made use of it. Many of the Confederates paid with their lives for their foolhardiness."*

Lt. Samuel C. Jones
22nd Iowa Infantry, Lawler's Brigade

Troops of the 22nd Iowa attacking the Railroad Redoubt

Col. Thomas Waul

Col. Charles M. Shelley

IOWA STATE MEMORIAL

Dedicated on November 15, 1906, the Iowa State Memorial is constructed of Vermont white granite in the style of a Greek-Doric semi-elipse. It features a mounted color-bearer with an unfurled flag awaiting orders to advance. Six bronze bas-relief panels depict Iowa soldiers participating in different portions of the Vicksburg Campaign.

Panorama of the Railroad Redoubt looking toward the Iowa Memorial taken in the early 1900s.

Col. Edmund Pettus

Lt. Col. Harvey Graham

Texas State Memorial

The Texas State Memorial was dedicated on November 4, 1961. The eleven steps leading up to the memorial honor Texas' sister states in the Confederacy. The memorial lists all of the Texas units on the defense line, in Johnston's Army and in Walker's Texas Division.

Constructed with Texas red granite

Yucca plant, native to Texas and the Southwest

The soldier looks in the direction of the counterattack made by Waul's Texas Legion, which drove the Union troops out of the redoubt.

Railroad Redoubt

Quiz Answers

1C 2A 3A 4B 5B 6C 7C 8B

Acknowledgments

TravelBrains sincerely thanks the following individuals and institutions for their contributions to the development of the Vicksburg Field Guide.

Special thanks to the Janitor, Rose, Thea, and the VA legal eagles. Without your support this would not have been possible.

Individuals

Virginia DuBowy
Elizabeth Dunn
Regina M. Goehring
Jeff Giambrone
Elizabeth Joyner
Mary Michals
Rachel Morris
Wayne Motts
Brent Smith
Larry Strayer
John White
Emma Lee Wilson
Terry Winschel
Frank Wood

Institutions

Chicago Historical Society
Chippewa Valley Museum
Duke University, Rare Book, Manuscript, &Special Collections Library
Frank and Marie-Therese Wood Print Collections, Alexandria, VA
Illinois National Guard and Militia
Historical Society
Illinois State Historical Library
Kentucky Historical Society
Library of Congress
National Archives and Records Administration
New York State Museum
Minnesota Historical Society
Missouri State Museum
Motts Military Museum
Old Courthouse Museum, Vicksburg, MS
State Historical Society of Iowa
State Historical Society of Missouri
The University of North Carolina at Chapel Hill
United States Army Military History Institute, Carlisle Barracks, PA
Vicksburg National Military Park
Wisconsin Veterans Musuem

Sound Design

Scorpio Sound

Music

Megatrax
Brent Smith using sample from the Ilio music library

Voice Actors - In order of Appearance

Audio Tour Narrator .... Reg Green
Audio Tour Guide .... Debby Winsberg
Audio Tour Historian .... Ed Bearss
Alice Shirley, Mary Loughbrough...............Angela Lee
Chaplain Foster, Pvt. Evans..................... Lance Smith
Capt. White...Terence Rae

Writers and Editors

Jack Chang

TravelBrains Vicksburg Team: Catherine Davis, Paul Davis, Ryan Gould

Book Photography Credits

Cover: Vicksburg National Military Park Vicksburg, MS, Library of Congress, Old Courthouse Museum, Vicksburg, MS. 5 "Battle of Champion Hill", Kurz & Allison, Rare Book, Manuscript, & Special Collections Library, Duke University, Durham NC. 6: MASS-MOLLUS/USAMHI, Carlisle, PA. 8: Vicksburg National Military Park. 9: MASS-MOLLUS/USAMHI, Old Courthouse Museum. 10-11: Library of Congress, Old Courthouse Museum. 12: Coonskin Tower courtesy Chicago Historical Society, Chicago, IL, Panorama courtesy Library of Congress, Cashire images courtesy Illinois State Historical Society, Springfield IL, MASS-MOLLUS/USAMHI. 13: National Archives. 14: Old Courthouse Museum, MASS-MOLLUS/USAMHI. 15: State Historical Society of Missouri, Columbia, MO. 16: Illinois State Historical Society, Thomas Smith Collection courtesy of L. M. Strayer. 17: MASS-MOLLUS/USAMHI, Old Courthouse Museum, Chippewa Valley Museum, Eau Claire, WI. 20 National Archives. 21: MASS-MOLLUS/USAMHI. 22: National Archives 23: Vicksburg National Military Park. 24: National Archives. 25: Library of Congress. 26: MASS-MOLLUS/USAMHI. 27: MASS-MOLLUS/USAMHI, Vicksburg National Military Park, National Archives. 28: Old Courthouse Museum, Library of Congress. 29: MASS-MOLLUS/USAMHI. 30 MASS-MOLLUS/USAMHI. 31: Ed Bearss, Vicksburg National Military Park. 32-33: Vicksburg National Military Park. 34-35: Library of Congress. 36: Old Courthouse Museum. 37: MASS-MOLLUS/USAMHI, Old Courthouse Museum. 37: 38 Vicksburg National Military Park, Larry M. Strayer Collection. 39: MASS-MOLLUS/USAMHI, Davis Library, Manuscripts Department, University of North Carolina, Chapel Hill, NC. 40: Frank and Marie-Therese Wood Print Collections, Alexandria VA, Vicksburg National Military Park. 42: Old Courthouse Museum, MASS-MOLLUS/USAMHI. 43: MASS-MOLLUS/USAMHI, Old Courthouse Museum. 44,45: F.D. Millet's 4th Minnesota Entering Vicksburg, Minnesota Historical Society. 46 Library of Congress. 47: Missouri State Museum, Jefferson City, MO, Frank and Marie-Therese Wood Print Collection. 48 MASS-MOLLUS/USAMHI, Old Courthouse Museum. 49: MASS-MOLLUS/USAMHI. 50. MASS-MOLLUS/USAMHI 51: Illinois State Historical Society, Illinois National Guard and Militia Historical Society, MASS-MOLLUS/USAMHI, New York State Museum, Albany, NY. 53: MASS-MOLLUS/USAMHI, State Historical Society of Iowa, Iowa City, IA. 54: MASS-MOLLUS/USAMHI, *Confederate Military History*, Vol. VII, Confederate Publishing Company, Atlanta, GA (1899), Library of Congress. 55: Confederate Military History, Vol. VII, State Historical Society of Iowa, Des Moines, IA.

Printed in Malaysia

The Modern Way to Experience the History of Vicksburg

6 Multimedia Modules

Battle — The Battle Module

Experience the Siege of Vicksburg from an extraordinary birds-eye perspective. For the first time, the Campaign and Siege of Vicksburg have been reconstructed with computer technology to give you an unparalleled animated picture of these historic events.

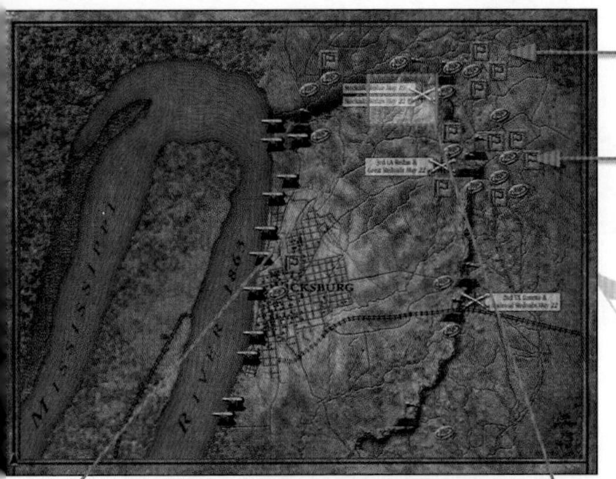

Interactive battle maps of the campaign, assaults and siege areas

Beautifully illustrated battle maps show historic terrain, buildings and roads

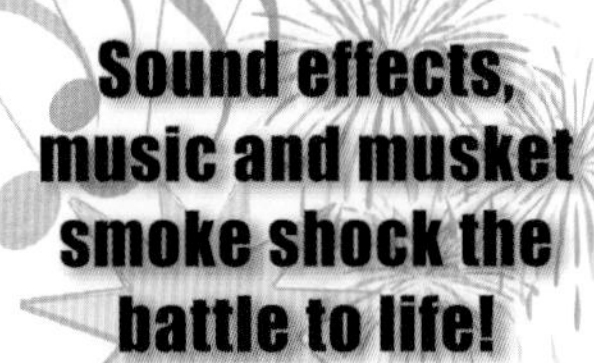

View the entire battlefield or zoom in for a close-up perspective

Detailed troop movements down to the regimental level

Famous battlefield landmarks like the Stockade Redan and the Great Redoubt

VCR-like controls let you play, pause, rewind and fast forward

With the click of a button you can overlay the modern day driving tour route to see where the TravelBrains' tour takes you

Numerous campaign and siege locations can be selected to view

Explore the biographies of the courageous soldiers who fought at Vicksburg.

Hear what the Siege of Vicksburg was like from the soldiers who were there. Audio recordings, made from the diaries of soldiers give you an extraordinary perspective of the struggle.

Take a Virtual Tour of the Battlefield

Experience the full grandeur of touring the Battlefield of Vicksburg with 17 QTVR panoramas of the Vicksburg National Military Park.

Explore famous landmarks like the Great Redoubt, the 2nd Texas Lunette, the Stockade Redan and more!

Use your mouse to look in all directions

COMPUTER DVD-ROM

THE MOVIE MODULE

The 35-minute animated movie is the perfect place to start your Vicksburg Expedition. It covers the history leading up to and including the siege, giving you a solid foundation to understand the historical context and significance of Vicksburg.

Learn about the events that shaped the Campaign and Siege of Vicksburg

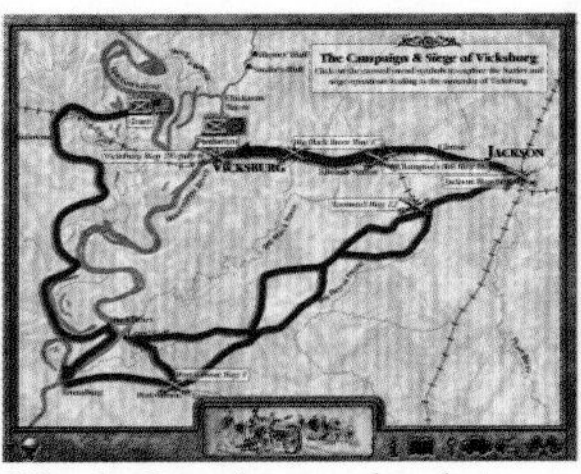

Watch Grant's army battle its way to the gates of Vicksburg

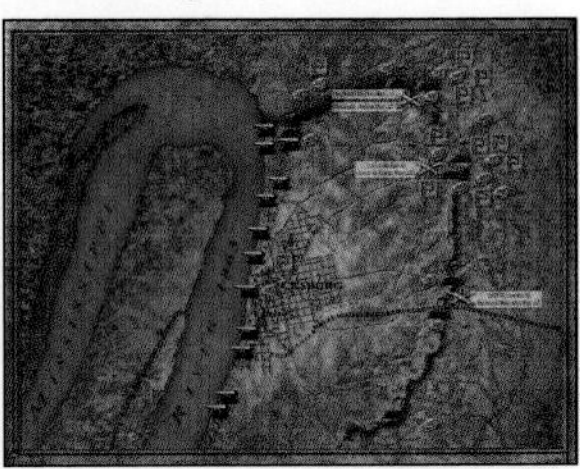
Watch a high-level overview of the siege

THE ARMIES MODULE

The Armies Module is the perfect place to learn about the commands of Pemberton and Grant. Short animated movies describe each army and their dispositions throughout the Siege of Vicksburg. If you are new to the subject, there's a movie that describes how a Civil War army was organized. For the Civil War buffs, there's a detailed order of battle with pictures of the commanders.

Movie describing the Army of the Tennessee

Movie describing the Army of Vicksburg

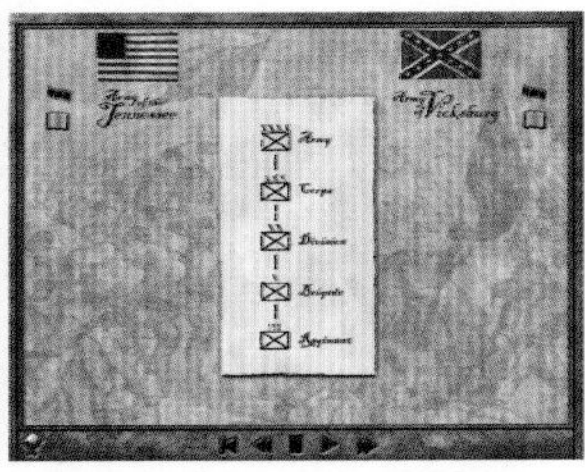
Movie describing how Civil War armies were organized

THE QUIZ MODULE

Play against another person or the computer. This fun quiz game will let you find out how much you really know about the Siege of Vicksburg.

The faster you answer, the more points you score!

Go head-to-head with a friend or solo against the computer

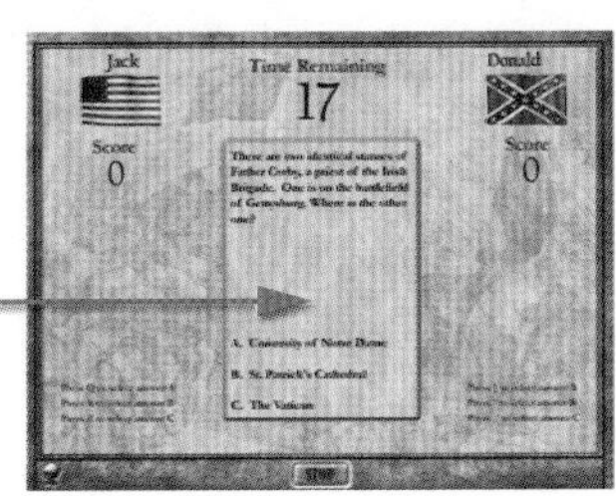

COMPUTER DVD-ROM

The Weapons & Tactics Module

The Weapons & Tactics Module explains the fighting methods used by generals and soldiers during the Civil War. It also includes a 3D museum that highlights some of the most common weapons used during the period.

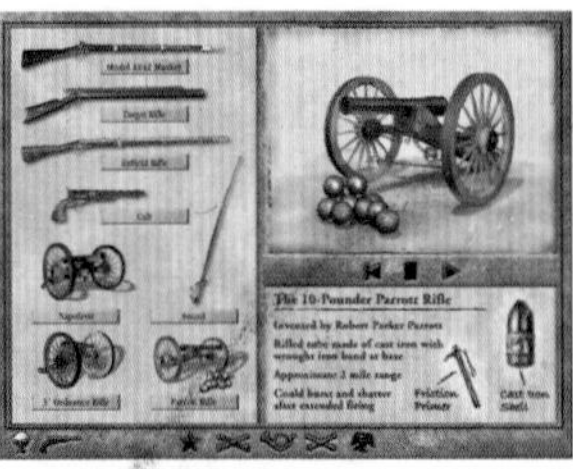
A 3D weapons museum lets you explore the weapons up close

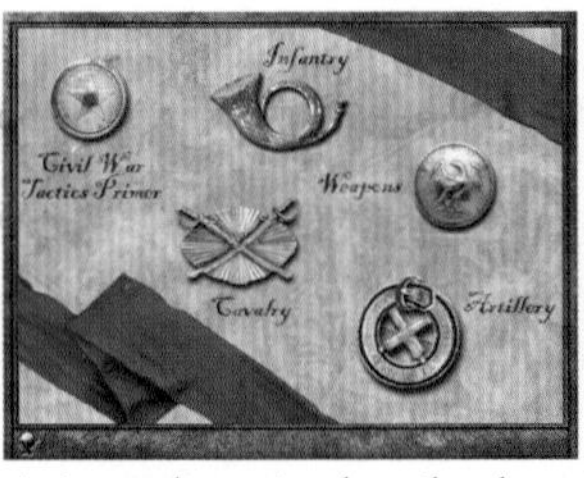

Animated movies describe the infantry, cavalry and artillery during the war

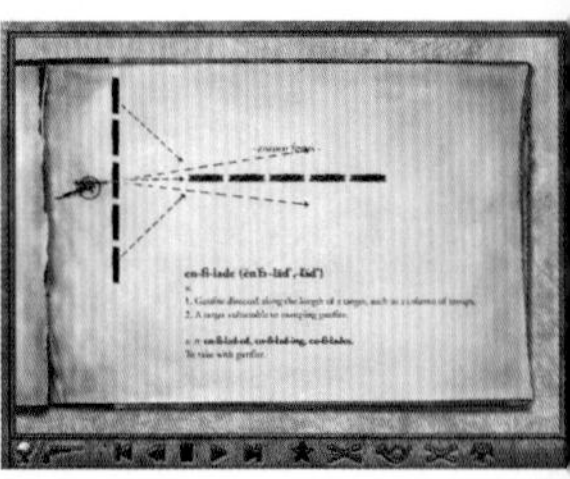
The tactics movie explains the changing nature of warfare and its effect on the Civil War

The Travel Information Module

This module contains the essential information and web sites you need to plan your trip to the battlefield.

DVD-ROM Minimum System Requirements

PC Minimum system requirements

OS:	Windows XP, Vista or later
CPU:	Pentium II 233 MHz processor or 100% compatible
Memory:	520 Mb RAM
Hard Disk Space:	50 Mb free hard drive space (uncompressed)
CD-ROM Speed:	8x DVD-ROM drive
Video card:	Capable of 16 bit color at 800x600 resolution
	Requires QuickTime 3.0 or greater (QuickTime™ 7.0 included)
	Requires Adobe Flash Player (Free download link included)
Sound card:	100% Windows compatible
Other:	100% Windows compatible mouse

Mac Minimum system requirements
Check at www.TravelBrains.com for the availability of a Mac compatable version of Vicksburg Animated